Belgrade to Buel
Football rivalries ~~ ~ ~~~
tight budget

By

Lee Colvin

Introduction

What do football rivalries mean to you? Do you wake up on the day of the game against your rivals with a weird feeling inside you? Do you have the horrible fear inside of getting beat? Well, that's what these games do to us all. No matter how old I get, I still get these feelings in the build-up to a match.

I've travelled to a few places to watch these games and have witnessed a lot of passion, hatred and commitment from the fans. Some rivalries are bigger than others, but your game is the biggest to you in your own mind.

Everybody loves their rivalry. When I was at school, if you played your nearest school you knew you couldn't lose as you would get slaughtered. Everybody has the same feelings worldwide. Winning these games is more of a relief than anything, and the fear of losing is gut wrenching. If you win, you can't wait to walk in to work/school on a Monday, but if you get beaten you go into hiding.

I'm not saying the games I've been to so far are the biggest. Some games that I picked were purely down to getting cheap flights for a particular weekend and finding a derby/rivalry. Some of these games involve teams from different cities or different countries, but most are derbies.

I've not been to many English rivalry games, but I hope to do so in the future. However, I'm an old-school football fan and it breaks my heart to watch an English derby/rivalry and see the daytrippers taking selfies and videos at crucial moments during games. Where do I start on half-and-half scarves for a derby? Big rivalries are about raw passion and exploding when there's a goal.

I could go into pages and pages of different teams' history and the politics of these games but I'm not going to. I think there are enough of those types of books out there explaining all this. I'm writing about my personal experiences of these games. The booking of cheap flights, the drama of games getting switched that completely messes the trip, and the buzz of trying to get match tickets for games that are complete sell-outs.

Some of these trips have been lads' trips and some have been as part of a weekend away with a partner. The things you do for a game of football, eh? This is my personal journey, from attending derbies in the late eighties right up to the current day. I work a normal Monday-to-Friday job and I've worked a lot of overtime to pay for some of these trips. Every game has been different but well worth it.

You may or may not agree with some of my views of these games, but enjoy the adventure and, who knows, there might be another book in the future. From getting baguettes thrown at my head in Madrid, blocks of ice in Buenos Aires, to getting soaked with beer in Rotterdam, this is my story.

Chapters

Buenos Aires

Boca Juniors v River Plate
Racing Club v Velez Sarsfield
(May 4/5th 2013)

Top tips for Argentina
Never book flights when you've had a few drinks.
Always factor in the crazy Argentina FA schedule changes.
Night Nurse is a great friend.
Never mention the Falklands.
When there is a happy hour from 7–10, drink normally.
Don't buy chewing gum with a big note.
Arguing with a taxi driver is never a good idea.
Cans of beer are a great weapon when thrown correctly.

It started with a drink…
    It was around November 2012, whilst having a pint in my local pub watching *Soccer Saturday,* that this trip came alive. Watching the scores on a Saturday afternoon, a few others and I were talking about derbies being played that weekend.
    I mentioned that one day I would go to the holy grail of football derbies, the Superclasico between Boca Juniors and River Plate. With usual lads' banter, I was told to 'keep on dreaming and get the fucking round in'.
    At this particular time in my life, I had just came out of an eight-year relationship and had got a loan to pay off a few bills that were left outstanding. To cut a very long story short, I had about a grand spare once I'd paid all my bills and it was sitting in my bank account on this particular Saturday afternoon.
    After a few more pints of Peroni, I was getting braver and decided to look at the next time Boca were playing River. It was scheduled for the end of April. A quick check on Skyscanner and I was booked

up for four nights. After a few more rounds of Peroni, I showed the lads who had called me a dreamer that I was on my way.

When I awoke on the Sunday morning with all my clothes still on and a stinking hangover, a big hazy thought occurred: I wasn't so pissed that I booked flights to Buenos Aires, was I? A quick panic to find my phone and check emails, and it was there in black and white to the tune of £700. Oh fuck, what have I done? That was one of the nicer thoughts going round my head at the time, to be honest.

I decided to text two good friends who had been to a few derbies with me, and asked if they were up for going? Both said I was 'off my fucking head', but they would think about it. One lad would have to try and have a nice chat with his wife about it. By mid-afternoon, to my relief, my two pals had both booked flights as I didn't fancy going to Argentina on my own. We were booked up and had a few months to get some cash sorted. What could possibly go wrong?

I had wanted to attend this fixture since I was a boy. Before the Internet and YouTube, I used to hear this game mentioned on *Transworld Sport* on a Saturday morning. The more I heard about this game, the more desperate I was to go. In 2004 *The Observer* newspaper had done a list of the top fifty sporting events to go to before you die: Boca v River was number one. This beats your Monaco Grand Prix and the Ashes. Buenos Aires has the highest concentration of football teams of any city in the world. When you add the factor of some of the best steak, red wine and a top derby into the mix, it makes a great trip.

Whenever I think of Boca Juniors, I automatically think of Diego Maradona. When I think of River Plate, I think of their El Monumental Stadium that was the home of the 1978 World Cup Final with all the confetti storms. Buenos Aires looked a great city to visit and has a great nightlife.

A couple of months after booking my travel, I noticed that there were two different dates for this game on two seperate weekends. It would cause us an enormous problem if the game was moved to May 5th. Our flights were booked for the previous weekend, which was the original date. After a few emails to the Argentina FA and a few ticket agencies, we were still none the wiser as they couldn't yet confirm either weekend. To say my arse was making buttons was an understatement.

At the start of January, I got an email telling me that the game was now confirmed for May 5th. After a few conversations with my two friends, we were stuck about what to do. We could stick with the original flights and watch River Plate at home in a run-of-the-mill league game, or try and change our flights. For me, this whole trip was about watching this once-in-a-lifetime game, so we agreed that we would change our flights to the following weekend, as long as it wasn't too expensive to do so. The company we had booked our flights with was the cheapest company on Skyscanner. That said, you get what you pay for was ringing in my head when they asked for £400 each way per person to change our flights. Our actual flight numbers were with Iberia so, after a search on their website, we found we could change our flights for £200, which was a big weight off our shoulders.

Now with our flights sorted, we just had the wee problem of sorting out match tickets. There are various agencies that cater for these games but they ain't cheap. We paid £200, and went with a company called Juancho Futbol, which was the cheapest. They arranged to pick you up before the game; also included in the price were a couple of beers and a slice of pizza. We would have liked to have got tickets through the normal routes but it was virtually impossible for a game of this size. After doing some research, it was clear that if you were going to attend this fixture once in your life then La Bombonera was the best stadium for atmosphere. Its stands are tight to the pitch and would very intimidating for opposing players.

So, on the Thursday before the game, Bertz, Adam and I set off for a few days of madness from Glasgow to Buenos Aires via Madrid. I must admit I felt really refreshed when we arrived in BA on the Friday morning. I never thought I'd say this, but after a dose of Night Nurse we got a great sleep. I'd felt much worse coming off a flight to Benidorm on a stag weekend.

After throwing our bags in the digs in the San Telmo district, we went for a mooch about as you do. The company that had our match tickets was only around the corner from our accommodation, so we thought we'd check that everything was okay and get our bearings for the Sunday-afternoon pick-up. After approaching this dilapidated building, I did start to panic that we had been scammed. All the way to Argentina and no tickets – surely not? A creaking door opened and, after a brief conversation with a lady who spoke much better English than us, we were assured everything was fine.

The San Telmo district was great for bars and for food; it was a bit edgy as well, so it felt like the perfect place to be. The first few bars we went into were quite friendly. Every TV was saying that Juan Riquelme would not be playing for Boca on Sunday due to injury. I'd seen this man play at his peak for Villareal and he's a class act.

We did a few touristy things and headed in a taxi to Rivers' El Monumental Stadium to get the official tour. As we were only going to be there for a few days, it was one of those things that we needed to tick off our list.

The rain started to bounce down while we were stuck in Friday afternoon traffic, and we did think about aborting the tour of the Monumental. Once we got moving and we passed a toll on the motorway, we attempted to pay our driver the fare in pesos. When we had arrived at the airport we'd got our currency from a cashpoint but it paid out in big notes. That caused an issue when our driver couldn't change any of them and started ranting at us.

We kind of got the jist of what he was saying and Bertz went in to a garage to get some change. He grabbed a pack of chewing gum and attempted to pay with this big note but the cashier just said, 'Have them for free.' It was like something out of a comedy sketch. As a kind local informed us, the driver was threatening us with the police. The police duly arrived and defused the situation by helping us get some change. Not a great start, by any means.

The tour of the stadium was done in Spanish, but we saw enough of this iconic arena to know about the history and the legends that had played there.

As we'd come off a long flight, we decided to stay awake as long as we could. When we saw a happy hours sign from 7–10pm in an English bar called Gibraltar, it was happy days. These happy hours sound great in theory, as you would buy a drink and then get a token to get another drink free. After buying five pints each and then getting another five pints free, we were steaming and talking a load of shite. Just like a normal Friday night, to be honest.

It's a bit similar to Spain in that people don't really go out until after 10pm. So while everybody was coming out and looking very smart, we were pissed and heading for our beds.

Adam had made contact via Twitter with a lad called Stuart, who stayed in BA, to see if he could get us tickets for Racing Club v Velez Sarsfield, which was being played on the Saturday night. We got a text on the Saturday afternoon confirming we had tickets for the game and we would be in the away section.

After sampling some unbelievable steak and a few beers while meeting Stuart, we were ready to head to the game. We headed to the Avellaneda area by train, whilst watching the pickpockets going about their business. I put my wallet alongside my balls as it was the only place I felt safe keeping it. To say that this wasn't a picturesque area is a bit of an understatement.

On our walk to the Estadio Presidente Peron, we were feeling pretty confident as we'd had a good few beers by this stage, but the number of police hanging around in their robocop outfits soon sobered me up. The streets were also lined with supporters' buses that looked like something from a bygone era; they didn't look like they could travel as far as the next street.

After a very stringent search, we were in the ground. The first thing that hit me was the smell of weed; it was Saturday night and there were a lot of stoned faces in the Velez Sarsfield section. The stadium was an old bowl-shaped one, but very atmospheric. Everybody was standing up and we decided to head left when we got to the top of the stairs. If we had turned right, we would have been in a pretty normal section but, having turned left, we were right in amongst their Ultras. These Ultras are not teenage boys who want to wave flags all through the game and then go home for a bedtime story. They are called Barra Brava, and every club in Argentina has them. They are battle-scarred lumps, have a lot of say in how their club is run and wield a lot of power. They control a lot of merchandise stalls, car parking, food stalls and ticket sales.

Within a few seconds of positioning ourselves towards the centre of the goal, we were approached in a roundabout sort of way by a big guy who wasn't messing about in asking who we were. Bertz had already grabbed my arm and said, 'Don't mention England.' We told him that we were from Scotland and were over for a few days. When he nodded at us and said, 'Ah, Scotland. Whisky, whisky,' I felt a bit safer, to be honest.

One guy did come up to us and started demanding we pay to stand amongst them. I had heard a few stories from tourists about this. Maybe it's on people's bucket list to stand in amongst the Barra Brava, but I wasn't sure if this guy was being serious or not. Anyway, we never paid.

As we stood out like sore thumbs, they must have thought we had balls of steel or were just plain fucking stupid. The truth was somewhere in between. They were singing all their songs and we bounced in tune to them and passed some of their banners down when they came above us. It was a great experience but I couldn't relax entirely. At one point before half-time, they were fighting each other towards the back of our section, which was a bit scary. We took a few pictures on our phones, which they weren't ecstatic about. In fact, Adam's arm was grabbed when he was taking a few pics and he was told not to take any pictures of their *capo* (leader).

Considering these two teams were supposed to be a starter to our main course the following day, it was a bouncing atmosphere around the ground. The actual football was a side issue for us. With around ten minutes of the game remaining, we gave each the other nod and left. The game ended up goalless.

Once in a taxi on the way to the train station, I felt relieved that we had survived and also learnt a few new songs, ha ha. The taxi driver bumped us for a few pesos but we didn't care as we just wanted out of the area.

The Saturday night in San Telmo was quite good, with most bars packed. Our bar played mostly British songs and attracted a good crowd, with backpackers kicking about all night. Floyd Mayweather was fighting but not many people were paying attention. We had learnt our lesson from the previous evening and were out at a normal time and mingling with locals. While in Argentina you are never too far away from one of Colombia's main exports either. Some of the prices that we were being offered were ridiculously cheap.

On Sunday I woke with a spring in my step. This was game day and this was what I'd talked about doing for years. I encountered a slight translation problem at the supermarket when I asked for a bottle opener at 8am to take back to my room for my wine. The guy just looked at me and opened my wine for me. I was planning on drinking it later, but here I was at 8am on a Sunday morning, walking about drinking a bottle of Malbec.

After breakfast, we headed off to get a few beers before our pick-up for the game. Whilst waiting for our minibus, we got chatting to French, Spanish and Brazilian lads who were on the same package as us. Bertz thought that it would be a great idea to get a case of beers for the bus. He came back with a load of cans but we were taken to a restaurant two streets away. Bertz' beers were left on the bus to get warm, while we had a few beers and pizza in the restaurant.

It was a nice sunny day but the sound of a police helicopter was never too far away. Whilst heading towards the ground, we were handed our match tickets which were season-ticket cards. These type of agencies get a block of tickets together. We were instructed not to talk too loudly whilst walking to the turnstiles, as the locals don't take too kindly to tourists taking tickets. Adam's ticket was the only one that didn't scan properly at the turnstile and we panicked. After a second attempt, it scanned fine. You could actually feel the tension in the air, even with more than two hours till kick-off.

Ideally we would have liked to mix in one of the many Boca supporters' bars and get the real build-up and atmosphere, but this was our only realistic option of getting three tickets together.

Once past the turnstile searches, we were in. It was still two hours to go but both ends were virtually full already. As luck would have it, we were only one block away from the River Plate section, which would be interesting to say the least. As it got nearer kick-off the volume cranked up a few notches, especially when the main Barra Brava group *la doce* (12th man) came into the stadium. La Bombonera is known as the chocolate box, and the noise goes right through you.

The teams emerged to a ticker-tape reception and it actually felt like the ground was vibrating. But within forty-five seconds River had scored a simple goal through Manuel Lanzini and it killed the atmosphere stone dead, to be honest. The River fans to our right-hand side were going crazy as expected, but it took a while for the ground to get the volume back up again. That all changed when Boca scored just before half-time through Santiago Silva, and the ground was bouncing once again. The fans were climbing up the high fences

10

behind both goals. I would have loved to have been in the bottom tier behind the goal as it looked mental.

The second half will probably live with me for the rest of my life; it was everything that this derby was supposed to be and more. There were two sendings off and the River coach also got sent off the pitch with a police escort. The game was abandoned for ten minutes as flares, little bombs and various objects were thrown at the River keeper. It seemed like a switch was turned on when the River coach, Ramon Diaz, was escorted off the pitch with riot shields. Four stands all went crazy with a planned display by fans dressed in ghost sheets with the letter B displayed everywhere; this was to remind the River fans of their relegation in 2011. This was Rivers first time at La Bombonera since then. The hairs on the back of my neck were genuinely standing up during this mad ten minutes. That feeling doesn't happen too many times in your life. The fans were sprayed with water to try and calm things down. I will take these moments with me to my grave.

As we were sitting close to River Plate fans, there were a lot of objects being thrown between the two sets of fans. A big block of ice landed very close to us and we also had the privilege of seeing a River fan lower his pants and show us his wedding tackle, which was very friendly of him. Our section responded by throwing small cans of non-alcoholic beer, which hurt if you felt the full force of them on your head.

The match came to an end in a one-each draw. In Argentina they definitely get one big thing right: they keep the home fans in the ground for half an hour and get the away fans out of the fucking road. It makes perfect sense but in Britain we do it the opposite way, which I don't understand.

Once the River fans had dispersed, we were let out in our group. It did have a school trip feel to it, if I'm honest, but we followed our tour guide back to our minibus and we went back to our digs for a quick change of clothes. The three of us were up for a heavy session; it had been a good day and we could struggle with a hangover all day on the Monday if we wanted.

We headed for a run-of-the-mill steakhouse, a little back-street place, and I got bang on the vino. After a decent meal we were ready to head to a bar, when the Scottish comedian Kevin Bridges appeared with a camera crew. They were in for some food but with us being Rangers' fans and him a Celtic fan, we had a friendly bit of banter with him and left.

After trying another bar, we headed back to our new local, the Gibraltar. Kevin Bridges was now in this bar as well. We had a good chat with him and he explained how he was at the game but staying for two weeks. With me being a Rangers' fan, I would love to say he was an arrogant arsehole but he wasn't; to be fair, he was a great lad. I'm not sure how he felt about bumping into three very pissed Rangers' fans though.

The next day every news bulletin was still talking about the game and all the incidents that had happened. When you saw it back on TV, you realised how mad that second half actually was. Bocas next home game had to played behind closed doors due to the madness from this fixture. A few weeks later an away fan was killed during a game, and all away fans were banned throughout the whole country. A very passionate country when it comes to football, although a bit extreme in some cases.

If I'm being honest, I did think we'd probably encounter some issues while in BA but the locals that we met were very friendly. There were certain areas where you had to have your wits about you, but that's the same in most cities. We really enjoyed the city and the whole experience. I'd recommend it to anyone.

'El Clasico'

Real Madrid v Barcelona
(21st November 2015)

Top tips for Madrid
Never give up hope of getting a ticket.
Always pay attention to handbags.
Beware of flying baguettes.

From the Superclasico to El Clasico. Now before you start saying this isn't a derby, I'm in total agreement with you. However this game has to be included because it's right up there as a massive rivalry. This game has gigantic appeal worldwide, and in recent years has been highlighted because of all its political connections. I could try and explain the full political situation between these teams, but I'd probably fill a different book with that.

In most people's eyes, Madrid is the flagship Spanish team and Barca represents Catalonia. That's where I'll leave that chat and concentrate on explaining about the weekend I attended this fixture.

When I was young and saw highlights of this game, it used to amaze me. When you think of some of the world's greatest players ever to kick a ball, then the majority of them have played in this fixture. On this particular weekend, Cristiano Ronaldo and Lionel Messi both took part. We all have different opinions about players but I think Messi is the best player in my lifetime.

I had been to both of their stadiums previously and, impressive as both are for their sheer size, the facilities are a bit basic compared to some of the new arenas we have. Santiago Bernabeu would be virtually full of Madridistas, with only a few hundred travelling Barcelona fans. This isn't a major thing in Spain regarding travelling supporters, as not many travel on most weekends during the season. The British, Germans and the Dutch have a different mentality to the Spanish.

The main problem revolved around how I was going to get a match ticket. All the usual ticket agencies had tickets available but at extortionate prices. I'm a sheet-metal worker and earn an average

13

wage; there's no way I'm paying a week's wages for a ticket. I know of people who have had a ticket for this game as a big birthday present, but the thought of paying around £400 pounds or more for the privilege made my stomach turn. I'd heard stories of people getting lucky on the day before the game at the Bernabeu ticket office, and that was an option, but there was no guarantee of getting one. There are always touts outside the ground but a lot of them can be fake.

I phoned the Madrid ticket office and was told to keep trying on the official site online, as some tickets do become available. I tried this for several days and was preparing myself to watch the match in a bar near the stadium. It's a bit like a gameshow when a few tickets get released – whoever hits the button first gets the prize. The seating plan comes up on the screen and then a circle appears when a ticket becomes available. The only thing in my favour was that the girl who was coming with me had no interest in football and had no intention of going to the game, so I just needed one brief.

On the Wednesday afternoon I tried again, in hope more than anything. After a couple of minutes I got through and purchased one ticket. The seat was in the north stand (fondo norte), section 429 behind the goal, and the face value was €145. My friend at work printed out my ticket with the barcode. After spending so long trying for a ticket, I was on my way and that piece of paper was now in my hand.

Travelling for this fixture was very easy compared to other games I'd attended. Me and my partner at that time, who was more of a good friend if I'm being honest, flew from Edinburgh to Madrid on the Friday morning. This wasn't your usual Friday morning flight to Spain, with stag and hen parties; it was full of Spanish people going home for the weekend or for business. Most people seemed to be reading about Saturday's big match, either that or they liked the look of Ronaldo's and Messi's legs.

Madrid is a great city for a weekend getaway. Yes, there's a lot of tourists, but it's nowhere near as much in your face as Barcelona. They are two completely different cities,in my opinion.Virtually every souvenir shop or newsstand had a picture of Ronaldo. We spent the Friday night in a few side-street bars just off the Gran Via. Most bars had the news on the TV, which was still telling horror stories from the Paris terrorist attacks the week before, and also doing a big preview of El Clasico.

Our hotel was within walking distance of the Bernabeu. The number of people that were over for this game was proof, if I needed it, that this game is a global phenomenon. A lot of news reports were saying that Messi might not be fit to play.

After a few drinks in the city centre, we decided to head up near the ground. Upon arrival, I couldn't help noticing the number of people looking for tickets. A few English actually had 'tickets wanted' signs held above their heads.

It was still around three hours before kick-off, so we headed to a nearby bar called The Irish Rover. It's a massive bar and had games from all over Europe on TV. It's a good meeting point, and the Madrid Ultras were dishing out their white T-shirts in there for the game. I was now comfortable and relaxed, having a beer and watching old clips of El Clasico games on a giant screen. Seeing Laudrup, Ronaldo, Figo, Stoichkov, Romario and many others, I got right in the mood.

The girl I was with went upstairs to the toilet and left her bag by her seat. Whilst she was upstairs, I answered a call on my phone, which turned into a very quick conversation when my pal realised I was abroad. I'm sure you've all got friends who panic when they hear an international dialling tone.

When she came downstairs, my friend asked where her bag was. I'd assumed she had taken it to the toilet with her, but it had been swiped in the few seconds of me answering the phone. I immediately informed the staff but the thief was well away. I felt anger, regret and hopelessness all at the same time. As it turns out, there wasn't much cash in there and she cancelled her cards straight away. The only problem was that her car keys were in there and her car was at Edinburgh airport. More about that later.

We had made plans in the morning that when I went to the game she would go to the hotel and chill out, as she wasn't interested in football. After speaking to an insurance company about her car keys, they told her she would need to report the theft to the local police and get a statement. As I walked her back to the hotel for a quick drink and to calm her down, we decided we would go after the game and report it. I was also told by the bar staff in The Irish Rover to come back after the game and they could maybe view the CCTV.

Due to the terrorist incidents in Paris the previous week, and with this being a major sporting event, I was expecting some security measures. I was a bit taken aback when there were police cordons stretched across the road half a mile from the stadium. The searches were as thorough as you'd expect, but there were three cordons to pass through. I hadn't exactly left myself lots of time to play with; with all the hassle, I was thinking I was maybe going to miss most of the first half. A few people were trying to surge forwards in the queues but I managed to get in just as the teams were arriving on the pitch. There was also an element of doubt in my head over whether the barcode would work off my works' printer. It was fine, though.

There was a massive French tricolor draped from one of the stands in a show of solidarity for the cowardly terrorist attacks. When I got to my seat, I was a bit shocked to see a guy wearing a Barca top only three seats away from me. Nobody was batting an eyelid, considering we were in a Madrid section. I could never imagine this happening in Istanbul, Belgrade or Glasgow.

I felt like a bit of a hypocrite because I was a tourist at this game, but there were people from all different parts of the globe sitting around me. It kind of doesn't feel real when Chinese fans are asking you to take a picture of them. It was a loud atmosphere but not an intimidating one; the Ultras behind the other goal were very lively and vocal, to be fair.

Barca really took control of this game and Suarez scored early on. The guy three seats away gave a little cheer but nobody said a word. Barca were running riot and it came as no surprise when Neymar netted a second just before half-time. The guy three seats away now started feeling braver and cheered a lot louder this time. A few of the locals didn't take kindly to this and started throwing a few verbals and baguettes in his direction. The only problem was that one of these fucking baguettes hit me in the fucking face. I wasn't too happy with the guy at this stage and shared a few verbals with him. I think everybody knew at half-time that there would be no way back for Madrid.

I was pretty sure that the Barca fan would disappear for the second half but, to his credit, he appeared at the start of the second half. I then witnessed a class act in Iniesta stroking the ball into the top corner. The whole stadium was applauding him, which I found very weird if I'm being honest, although when you realise what he's done in his career, and that he scored the winning World Cup Final goal for Spain, it made sense. Again, you wouldn't see this in many other big games around the world.

Messi then came off the substitutes' bench and controlled the tempo, before Suarez added another goal. There was also a red card for Madrid with five minutes to go, but I was already heading to The Irish Rover at that stage to see if they had any news about the bag. It turned out that they weren't interested. I got talking to a local, and he said, 'It's an easy location for pickpockets and bag thieves.'

The girl who was with me had decided to head to the police station and report the theft while the game was on. So while I was sitting watching the game having a baguette slapped on my face, she was catching a metro to a local police station. Not the greatest of days and I still felt guilty that the bag had gone. We both had a nice meal and some wine that night, but not too much as we had an early flight back to Edinburgh.

The spare keys were at her flat in Glasgow but couldn't be found so, after arriving back in Edinburgh, we couldn't get the car out of the car park. The AA came out and opened it just in case the spare set were inside, but they weren't. Her mom and dad drove us back to Glasgow and the keys were found under a fruit bowl. Her friend had looked everywhere but not there. Now I'm always paranoid about handbags being left alone.

This fixture is purely about the game and the quality that was on show. So, my lasting memories of watching some of the world's best players are of a baguette and a set of keys.

Madrid:
Navas, Ramos, Varane, Marcelo, Danilo, Bale, Kroos, Modric, Benzema, Ronaldo, Rodriguez. Subs:Isco, Pepe, Carvajal, Casilla, Jese, Casemiro, Kovacic

Barcelona:
Bravo, Mascherano, Pique, Alba, Alves, Busquets, Iniesta, Rakitic, Suarez, Neymar, Roberto Subs: Messi, Adriano, Mathieu, El Haddadi, Ramirez, Vermaelen, Stegen

Ticket stubs

Feyenoord lads

Feyenoord v Ajax

Hamburg v St Pauli

Norn Iron fans in Dublin

Red Star v Partizan

View from the away section at Racing v Velez

Full time tourists at the Bombonera

Sporting v Benfica

Ticket stubs

The worst looking boyband in Belgrade

River Plate fans on the top tier

BELGRADE

FK Crvena Zvezda V FK Partizan
(26th November 2011)
'Eternal Derby'

Top tips for Belgrade
Take a very, very, very warm coat and hat if visiting in November.
Don't go out on a student night when you have an early-morning flight.
Don't look for a venue playing S Club 7 songs.
Don't ask current footballers to take a picture of you with a legend.
No pyro, no party!!

This was one derby that interested me very much. The Eternal Derby has a certain edge to it, and makes a great spectacle off the park. There aren't any real political connections between the two clubs but it's a game where you need to have your wits about you, and there isn't a half-and-half scarf in sight.

When planning this trip, we decided to go to the match at the Marakana (Red Star Stadium) as it's a bigger stadium and it would be easier obtaining tickets. After reading various reviews, we knew we could get tickets over there without any major problems.

After looking at our various travel options, we decided Glasgow to Belgrade via an overnight stay in Luton was the best for us. We flew down to Luton at 7pm on the Thursday and had booked a hotel for one night in the centre. The plan was to have a few beers in Luton and get a good sleep before our 7am flight to Belgrade. Our morning taxi was ordered, so what could possibly go wrong?

Let's be honest, a few beers never ends up being just a few beers, does it? After a couple of drinks, it was soon apparent that it was student night and, with various drinks promotions, you were looking at a pound a drink wherever you went. Being the last people out of a nightclub at 3am was not on the agenda. Adam had retired to his room around midnight but was woken by us singing whilst munching on kebabs as we walked up the street.

Our taxi arrived at 5am as planned, but we were nowhere near ready. After a quick chat with our driver, he gave us five minutes max as he had other pickups. With barely a wink of sleep Adam, Bertz, Craig, Ross and I headed to the airport, not exactly in great health. The queue was out the door and if we hadn't purchased fast-track tickets, we would never have made the flight. Once on the plane, we were all spark out before we had taken off.

On arrival in Belgrade I felt the cold instantly; it was Baltic. The taxi driver assured us that there was no way the game could possibly get called off due to the weather. Heading into the city, you couldn't help but notice that some of the areas looked very rough and there was still a lot of poverty in this part of Serbia.

We had an apartment for the weekend in the Silicon Valley part of Belgrade. There are a few decent bars and restaurants around this area; it's not overloaded with tourists so we were paying what all the locals were paying, which is always a bonus.

We headed over to the Marakana in two taxis to get our match tickets. Our taxi driver was telling us that it was a certainty that Red Star would win comfortably. He was a Red Star fan, though. After telling him we were from Glasgow, he asked us if Dunfermline would win the following day. We couldn't tell him who they were playing but he knew everything about them and their opponents, and all the statistics. He bets on all the football leagues in Europe except the Serbian one, as he says it's corrupt and people take bribes.

There was a small queue at the ticket booth but worryingly some people were walking away shaking their heads. My knowledge of Serbian is very limited at best, but I knew that these people weren't happy. After a quick enquiry, we were informed that the North Stand was completely sold out. This is the main section behind the goal where the legendary Delije (heroes) Ultras stand. We purchased tickets for the West Stand, which we were told was a bit safer. The cost was around ten pounds, once we had converted the Serbian dinar.

After a walk around the stadium, with the groundsman letting us in for a short while, we were told that there was a bar in the West Stand that was open for beer and food. There were a few people connected to Red Star wearing suits, and also a few journalists in this bar which overlooked the pitch.

While sinking a few of the local LAV beers, we noticed a living legend come walking into the bar. This man, Robert Prosinecki, was the current manager of Red Star and was one of the best players in the world in the 1990s. Real Madrid, Barcelona and a European Cup winner with Red Star in 1991 are all on his CV. We recognised him instantly and asked a guy wearing a Red Star tracksuit to take a picture of us, which he wasn't overjoyed at doing.

The people who worked at the stadium were great and couldn't do enough for us. The commercial manager offered us discounts in the club shop but we were more interested in getting on the booze and exploring the Friday night scene in Belgrade, although Adam did buy a fridge magnet, ha ha.

After hitting a few bars, we threw Craig into his bed as he was talking Chinese at this stage and none of us could understand him. We went to Vanilla nightclub where MTV Serbia were filming. The place was totally packed and lively.

Ross said, 'Let's go somewhere else, this is all Serbian music.'

I was pissing myself laughing when he said that. I asked him, 'Do you want S Club 7?' Imagine a nightclub in Serbia playing Serbian music on a Friday night, cheeky bastards! After a few more drinks in a different club, we headed back to the apartment totally done in.

Saturday morning and we were recovering in the apartment. There was a big press conference on the TV, which was talking about the derby. One of the players getting interviewed looked very familiar; it was one of Red Stars players and it was the very same player who'd growled at us while taking our picture with Robert Prosinecki the day before. It's like somebody asking Messi to take a picture of you with Maradona, I suppose, on a much, much smaller scale.

The game kicked off at 6pm, so we had plenty of time for food and beers. We were drinking right in the centre of town but didn't see any football colours during the day, which felt strange. As it was starting to get dark, we got two taxis over to the ground and this is when my adrenaline started kicking in. To say there was a heavy police presence was an understatement. We could only get so far in our taxis due to the traffic; we were in the Red Star area and it felt very edgy. There were groups of lads hanging out who weren't exactly waiting for an invite to a tea party. They weren't small lads, either – I don't think we saw a small Serbian all weekend.

Bertz had told me to say I was from Glasgow if anybody asked, and not to mention fucking England. With him saying that, my arse did start to twitch; you only have to think back to the early 1990s and these people were involved in a war.

We made our way up the hill to the West Stand and past the lines of robocops. The commercial manager saw us and remembered us from the previous day. He must have been very happy that we bought one fridge magnet between us. To be fair to him, he did step in when the steward taking our tickets at the entrance didn't understand that we wanted to keep them as a souvenir.

Once inside, we made our way to our seats. I say seats, but they were like the ones at the old Wembley stadium with no backs on them; the dollops of bird shit didn't make them appealing to sit on either. The facilities were not great but we were there for the atmosphere and whatever else.

It was thirty minutes before kick-off and the East Stand opposite was packed in one section with a proper firm of Partizan. They have various Ultra groups but their main one is the Grobari (Gravediggers). So Partizan, being the away team, had roughly a third of the East Stand, the full section of the South Stand and a third of the West Stand.

To be honest, we weren't there to see the quality of the football. Like a lot of clubs in Europe these days, the idea is to bring youngsters through the ranks and sell them for a profit to a team from a bigger league. Watching the Partizan keeper trying to get back down the tunnel after his pre-match warm up was an event in itself. Firecrackers were being launched from all angles. When the two teams emerged from the tunnel it felt like the whole stadium was covered in smoke. Firecrackers engulfed the arena and it was a full-on pyrotechnics' show from both sets of supporters. If this had been in the UK, the Health and Safety executive would have had an heart attack. You can see why visiting European teams come here and crumble as it's a very intimidating arena. Although there is a running track around the pitch, it takes nothing away from the atmosphere, which isn't the case at some different venues.

Both teams started at like a hundred miles an hour, but the quality on the park wasn't the best. Lots of passes were misplaced but, in a frenzied atmosphere, that was to be expected. Red Star got a penalty and failed to score. However, the game did get stopped a few times as the Partizan fans decided to throw fireworks onto the pitch and several were also aimed at the police, who were protected by their shields. The fire brigade are well experienced at this fixture and were constantly putting out flames. When this happened, the pitch was covered in fog for a few minutes.

It was scoreless at half-time but, after trying to get through the tunnel to the safety of the changing room, Partizan gave up and had their team talk at the dugout area. A few of their players had managed to get down the tunnel but when the hail of missiles increased they waited and rejoined their team mates a few minutes later. Nobody around us batted an eyelid. This would be front-page news back at home for a week. We were standing up roughly between the halfway line and eighteen-yard box towards the Partizan section.

The teams started the second half in similar fashion to the first in a very scrappy game. I found myself watching the crowd rather than the game, as there was always something happening. It felt like I was a seven-year-old boy again.

Partizan scored twice in the second half through Vukic and Scepovic to run out 2–0 winners. The more the game went on, the more you got used to the pyro from the stands. We never witnessed any violence between the two sets of fans at the game, but you could tell that it could kick off at any moment even with the number of police around. It also felt strange to see police separating the different groups of Partizan supporters, although there is a lot of internal fighting between them. They still managed to toss aside their differences to chant hatred to the Delije at the opposite end.

We walked back into the city centre, as every bus or tram looked absolutely mobbed. After finding a decent steakhouse, we were getting ready for a few beers before our crazy flight back to Luton at 4.30am. When booking this trip, the flight time had seemed fine but, having been drinking for most of the day and having a Saturday night in some lively bars, it wasn't ideal. As we were getting into the swing of Saturday night, I think we all wanted to stay but Belgrade doesn't have lots of options for getting back to the UK. So, after our flight arrived back in Luton, we had a few hours to kill before our flight back to Glasgow.

I would definitely recommend going to this Eternal Derby. A great atmosphere, with the pyro adding to the occasion. Belgrade is a decent place for a weekend away; ideally I would go back when it's a bit warmer, and go to the game at Partizan's stadium. All in all, a good trip that went smoothly for a change.

Rome

Lazio v Roma
(16th November 2008)
'Derby della Capitale'

Top tips for Rome
Be prepared to witness violence.
If taking a female partner, make sure they don't need the toilet while the game is on.
Be prepared for people trying to steal your tickets at hotels.
The Curva Nord isn't a relaxing place for a Sunday evening.
When in Rome…

I'd heard a lot about this derby; I'd been told it was by far the biggest derby in Italy. If I'm being completely honest, this was my type of game. There's a lot of hatred and the games always have an edge to them. Although these teams have both won the Scudetto, and continue to challenge most years, the prize is to be the top dog in the city. Lazio last won the title in 2000, and Roma won it the following year in a golden period for the city. As in Milan, these two teams share the same stadium, but this is a different rivalry altogether.

I must admit to having had a soft spot for Lazio when I was younger, mainly due to Paul Gascoigne playing for them. I remember watching him score in the derby with a header, but the things that stood out for me were the big displays before the game and all the colour and atmosphere. At that time in the UK there weren't any tifo displays so that really made an impression on me. There has been a lot of controversy over the years about these displays and banners, but there is no denying they add to the occasion. If you were to ask your friends to pick some of the best derbies in Europe, then this game would be up there with them.

There were various ways of getting tickets but I didn't want to go over and wait until the last minute to source them. Lazio had started the season pretty well and this had the potential to be the biggest game between them for a long time. After quite a lot of searches online, I came across a company that offered tickets that were not much dearer than the face value. They also promised that they would deliver the tickets to our hotel. I always get paranoid about these type of arrangements because of the number of people that get scammed but, after a bit of searching, they seemed legit. I could have picked any section in the stadium but I picked the infamous Curva Nord, which is the Lazio section behind the goal. When in Rome, as they say. I was also selling this weekend away to my partner as a nice, relaxing, cultural weekend away.

The travel itinerary was fairly straightforward, flying out from Stansted on the Saturday morning and returning back Monday, with the game played on Sunday evening. After arriving at Ciampino Airport at midday, I couldn't believe how warm it was for mid-November. It was good to be walking around with a T-shirt on, although the locals were wearing thick coats. Walking about with a map upside down and a T-shirt on, surprisingly enough they probably had me marked down as a tourist.

I was informed by the ticket company that my tickets would be waiting for me at my hotel, which was just by Termini train station. At the check-in, the guy told me no tickets had been delivered. Much as I wanted to see the sights of Rome, the main part of this trip for me was the fucking derby not the Colosseum. The guy asked a few other members of staff but there was no joy. At this point I'd sent a few panicky emails to the ticket agency, as there wasn't a contact number to get hold of them. Had I made a schoolboy error and fallen for the oldest trick in the book? With the Italian authorities now being very strict about purchasing tickets, with identification needed and your names on the tickets, I couldn't just turn up outside and try and get the briefs. Plus I'd already paid for them some three months earlier.

I don't want to go all Judith Chalmers on you, but Rome is a very nice city. There's quite a lot to see and do and some of the sights are on a lot of people's must-see lists. I couldn't help but wonder at how friendly the local people were, yet in twenty-four hours there was the potential of mayhem at the derby.

After a relaxing Saturday afternoon of being a full-time tourist, I still had not heard from the ticket agency. All I could do was play the waiting game and hope they contacted me. Anyway, a few large glasses of vino always make most of my problems disappear.

36

We spent Saturday evening at Piazza Navona, which is a great spot with plenty of lovely restaurants. I was called by an unknown number; it was a guy from the agency and his words, that the tickets were definitely at the hotel and they were lying bastards, reassured me in a way. He arranged to meet me at the hotel reception the following morning to sort this mess out.

He arrived bang on time, introduced himself and told me that if they didn't find the tickets then his pals would come over later and smash the fucking place up. A bit extreme, but I wanted my tickets and I left it up to him to talk to the front desk. He had delivered the tickets on Thursday evening and exchanged a bit of football banter with the member of staff who he gave them to. After explaining this, the envelope with the tickets miraculously appeared in a drawer right under their noses. I'm certain they had tried that very same drawer the day before. I was grateful to him for sorting it out, but I don't know if it was a genuine mistake by the hotel staff or not.

All the coffee shops and bars had the TV on, and all the talk was about the derby. I was looking forward to this more so than the Milan Derby, purely because everyone had told me that it was crazy. There wasn't much sign of colours during the day, and the majority of tourists hanging around the Trevi Fountain were probably not aware of the game, but as it started to get dark I was right up for the game.

We got the tram over to the Stadio Olimpico and got off by the notorious Ponte Duca D'Aosta bridge. This has the River Tiber running through it. Many British football fans may have had the misfortune to be near this bridge, as it's a spot where Italian fans have stabbed many foreign supporters over the years. I'm not a legal expert but most of these stabbings get the equivalent fine of us pissing in the street back at home, and it's called a 'pinch' in Italy.

It was pitch black and it was starting to feel a bit edgy. I hadn't seen any Lazio colours yet, but a lot of people were casually dressed and blending in. There were a few café-type bars just to the right of the bridge, and we headed there for a few Peronis, with just over two hours until kick-off.

While sitting at the bar I could sense that something was happening. I've seen a few brawls at football games and the group that was starting to form outside this bar was growing in number. My partner thought I was being a bit paranoid but I knew something was going down. After about ten minutes, a shout went up from the crowd and they covered their faces with scarves and started to run round to the Lazio section.

As football stadiums goes, this must be one of the most impressive areas outside a stadium I've ever seen, with tree-lined streets and statues of Olympians thrown in for good measure. What was now apparent was the sound of police sirens filling the air and police running to where this battle was taking place. It had obviously been pre-arranged and the sound of hundreds of bottles getting smashed was also worrying. When walking over to the turnstiles I did start to panic for a while as I had my partner with me. I'm sure the promise of a relaxing weekend was going through her head. The two groups were still fighting outside but the police were starting to seperate them. It was a relief just to get inside the ground at that point.

A simplistic way of explaining this hatred would be to say that Roma are left-wing and Lazio are right-wing. That wouldn't be a clear picture to be honest; there are a lot of fascist and anti-fascist views and these can be seen in some Ultra displays. Lazio are seen as the team from the outskirts of Rome, and Roma are seen as the team from the city, with more fans. They both hold a lot of anti-government displays and sometimes share a common view.

Fair play to the guy from the ticket agency; he knew when I booked these tickets that my partner was coming to the game and he got us tickets for the very back of the Curva Nord. This was much safer than being at the front where it looked fucking crazy. There is a fence that splits the Curva Nord but when we were making our way to our seats people were climbing over it to get access to the middle section to join in with the Irriducibili Ultras. The Curva Sud opposite was bouncing as well. As the Stadio Olimpico was hosting the 2009 Champions League Final, a lot of improvements had been made to the stadium.

As you can imagine, when the two teams came out to start the game the noise was unreal, but something strange happened after the kick-off. The Ultras from both teams were silent for several minutes and I couldn't get my head round it. I later found out that Lazio Ultra Gabriele Sandre had been shot dead in November 2007 by a policeman when travelling to a game. Both Ultra groups had agreed on silence for a few minutes as a show of respect for this poor twenty-seven-year-old lad. They all had banners with Gabriele's face on them. It seemed bizarre that I'd witnessed these groups fighting outside less than an hour ago, but they were now paying their respects together inside.

If I'm being completely honest, I wasn't paying much attention to the actual game unless the play was up at our end. There were various different groups fighting each other at the front of the section; it was a bit worrying, but calmed down after a few minutes. Being served drinks up at the back was a nice little bonus, though.

I recognised more of the Roma players than Lazio. Panucci and De Rossi stood out, but the living legend Francesco Totti didn't look too bad either. While Lazio didn't have any great household names, they had a much more youthful side, played with a lot of energy and were unlucky not to score on several occasions. Ten minutes before half-time, my partner decided she needed the toilet. How we were going to get down there was a problem. The stairways weren't clear and we had to force our way down slowly; we eventually got to the toilets ten minutes later, which wasn't ideal but could have been worse.

During half-time, a group of Lazio decided to steam in to the Roma supporters in the Tribuna Tevere stand to our left. There were a few punches thrown from both sides and a few were getting skelped with belts. After a few charges at each other, the police decided to stop it, then the teams came out to start the second half. It was unreal; it was like the police decided to let the fans have a little play at the interval and then, before the rest of the watching world came back, they decided enough was enough.

Julio Baptista scored the only goal of the game just after the break and there was also a red card for each team. The Ultras from both teams made the game for me. Although football-wise there wasn't much between the two teams, it was a great experience with the stadium virtually full.

We didn't see any trouble after the game and quickly got a bus back to Termini. After the trouble before the game and at half-time, I thought the papers the next day would be full of images of these incidents but I found just a little column about it in *La Gazzetta dello Sport*. Part of me thinks that this was deliberate due to Rome hosting the Champions League final later in the season. If it had been in the UK, it would have been front-page news with threats of various sanctions.

Roma finished the season a few places above Lazio, to remain the top team in Rome. My advice would be to attend this derby as it's up there with some of the best, especially with a full stadium. When in Rome…

Genoa

Genoa v Sampdoria
(3rd February 2014)
Derby della Lanterna

Top tips for Genoa
Never trust the Italian fixture list.
Never underestimate fan power.
Never take notice of a drunken friend's speech.
Always pay attention to taxi drivers.
Drinking Screwdrivers all day is bad for you.

Once upon a time I was a football fan and booking trips was easy and everything went to plan. This wasn't one of those trips.

At the start of 2014, few pals and I were looking for a weekend away with a good derby and a good atmosphere. Genoa ticked all the boxes and, with cheap flights to Milan, it was booked. This derby is very rarely sold out, so tickets would be easy to get once we were over there. I had stayed in Genoa before in 2000, whilst travelling to watch Rangers in a Champions League game in Monaco, and knew it was a decent place to visit.

Stadio Luigi Ferraris is an iconic stadium, one that really stood out for me during Italia 90. Scotland played two games there during this tournament and I can remember running home from school to watch them get beaten by Costa Rica in a sun-drenched stadium. The four corners made it different to anywhere I'd ever seen before and the stands were very close to the pitch, which was unusual at that time in Italy. It looked an intimidating venue with a tight pitch, and always had a great atmosphere. In the early nineties, with Italian football on Channel Four, I saw the stadium regularly and would see Lombardo, Platt, Vialli and Mancini strutting their stuff. The only real standout player for Genoa from that era I could remember off the top of my head would be Tomas Skuhravy.

Although both teams share this stadium, Genoa were the home team so we would be purchasing tickets for the home section. Genoa were to have roughly sixty to seventy percent of the ground. The one

41

thing that stood out about this game was the atmosphere. Let's be honest, the way football is in the modern era then Genoa and Sampdoria are never going to win the league unless some tycoon gets bored and buys one of them. I know Samp won the league in 1991, but things have completely changed financially in football. This game is like their two cup finals every season. The more I looked into this game, the more I read about the atmosphere being one of the best in Italy, despite no real trouble.

This game was originally scheduled for Sunday evening on 2nd February. With this in mind, we booked Edinburgh to Milan on the Friday morning, returning Monday afternoon. The train journey from Milan to Genoa would take us roughly two hours.

Around a week before the game, the TV companies decided to make this fixture a 12.30 kick-off on Sunday lunchtime. This did not go down well with all the various supporters groups, who were threatening to boycott the game. The unique selling point of this derby was its atmosphere and it wouldn't be the same at that time of day. When you add into the mix that there was a big market in Genoa on at that time, and Italy is still a very religious country, then you kind of understood where they were coming from. For the rest of the week, officials from both clubs were adamant that the game would have to be played on Sunday lunchtime. The Ultras from both teams were threatening violence if it went ahead.

After a chat with my pals who were coming on this trip, we decided we would be scabs and still attend the fixture, although with not many fans there it wouldn't be great. Our flight was at 7am and my alarm was set at 4am for the drive to Edinburgh airport. These flight times always sound easy when you book them, but when your alarm is going off at a stupid time I sometimes think why the fuck am I doing this. I also said that I wasn't drinking until I got to Genoa but that went out the window at half five in the airport bar. The breakfasts at airports would make most people turn to drink.

Once we'd arrived in Milan and got to the main train station, we got a carry-out and we were on our way. Within ten minutes of being on the train, the snow was getting heavy; for a split second we thought we had a got on a train to Geneva rather than Genoa. It turned out that we were on the right train and once we got near to Genoa the weather was quite normal, which was a relief.

On arrival, we got a taxi to our hotel and shared a bit of banter with our driver who was wearing a Sampdoria hat. In his broken English he was muttering the word Monday to us. Adam, Craig, John and I didn't have a clue what he was talking about and just nodded at him.

Once we'd checked in and had a few beers, we went to get our match tickets. There was a Genoa club shop down at the harbour which sold match tickets. When we arrived, there was quite a big queue, but after waiting a while and getting our passports photocopied by the staff, we had our tickets. With it now being Friday afternoon, we stayed down at the harbour and had a good few relaxing drinks. With Genoa being a port, there are plenty of bars and restaurants and a fairly lively nightlife compared to other parts of Italy.

When we got back to the hotel to get changed, I asked Adam why there had been a queue when we were getting tickets. Were the fans protesting about the game? Whilst he was looking at our tickets he shouted, 'OH FUCK!!'. The game had now been switched to Monday evening and it said this on the tickets. It had been switched on the Friday morning while we were on a plane, and it now made sense what our taxi driver had been trying to tell us.

As our flight back was on Monday afternoon, my first reaction was to look for flights back home asap. How the fuck could a game due to be played on Sunday get changed on the Friday? There was nothing else we could do other than go out and have a good Friday night.

We did a bar crawl on Via San Lorenzo, and then Adam gave us a William Wallace style speech. His wife had given him the nod to stay an extra night and go to the game and his, 'We're here now we may as well stay,' speech certainly convinced me. I was up for it but John and Craig were adamant that they were going back on the Monday afternoon flight.

Once we surfaced on the Saturday morning, the attitude had changed about the game and we exchanged our tickets at the shop with a full refund. Once we had got some food inside us we all felt better, but the longer the day went on and the more beers I consumed led me to change my mind. I told the lads I was going to stay an extra night for the match. That comment 'We're here now we may as well stay' was stuck in my head. In the back of my mind I thought at least one of them would stay with me.

To say we were pissed on the Saturday night is like asking whether Jordan has a pair of tits. It's actually quite scary how much you can drink on these trips.

With a stinking hangover on the Sunday morning, I asked the lads one last time who was staying but no one was up for it. I phoned work to tell them I needed an extra day's holiday and went back to the club shop and got the cheapest ticket possible. I also had to change my flight to the Tuesday afternoon as well; all this for a fucking game of football.

As we had a day to kill we went over to the Luigi Ferraris stadium and got a few pictures. On one of the walls outside there was graffiti saying 'Derby Alle 12.30, Derby Di Sangue'; roughly translated, this means that if the derby kicks off at 12.30, there will be blood.

We visited a trattoria right by the stadium. It was a nice little place with locals all watching the football on the TV and having a nice relaxing Sunday afternoon drink. For some unknown reason in my head, I decided I hadn't drunk enough on this weekend and ordered a Screwdriver cocktail. The lads eventually started drinking these as well and a quiet Sunday afternoon turned into carnage. We got chatting with a few locals and they invited me to come down before the game on Monday evening.

The next thing I know is that I'm in bed, it's Monday morning, the room is full of McDonald's bags and the lads are packing their bags. I wasn't capable of climbing out my bed, never mind going home with them.

Once they had gone, I got another hour's sleep before having to check out and then check into a smaller place round the corner as our hotel was full with business people. After three days of solid drinking I looked a complete mess, but I was determined to go to this game.

It was a really slow day and I couldn't even look at a drink. Late afternoon the rain started getting heavier; if the game was called off now, I'd have been as well just jumping in to the sea and calling it a day. I knew the lads would slaughter me when I got back if it was off.

I feared the worst as I started walking to the stadium along the Bisagno river bed. It was about a twenty-minute walk and I noticed that both sets of fans were mixing. I walked past the trattoria that we'd been in on Sunday but I gave that a big swerve as I was running on empty and couldn't look at another Screwdriver.

Once I was past the ticket searches and finally in the stadium, I could relax in the knowledge that the game was definitely on. Although I was situated in the corner, my view was decent enough. The Genoa Ultras were just to my left in the north section. This ground had hardly been touched since the 1990 World Cup and the facilities were basic, but I really liked it. The displays from both sets of fans were different class. From a distance the Sampdoria one looked slightly better in my opinion; all that was missing was Lombardo.

Both teams started the game at a frenzied pace and there were chances at both ends. It felt like a real local derby as there wasn't many foreign accents to be heard, apart from mine. When you take into consideration this game had only been rescheduled three days prior to this, then the attendance of 30,000 was great. The stadium only holds around 36,000.

I'm not going to lie and say the standard on the park was fantastic because it was far from that. Lopez scored a simple goal after twenty-four minutes and the flag-waving Samp Ultras celebrated like they had won the league. The Genoa fans really tried hard to lift their team but I couldn't see them scoring in a million years. You could see why these teams had been pretty much mid-table for a while. But, like most of these games, the quality of the football was a minor detail. I was there for the atmosphere and I would say that, if anything, this game is underrated.

Sampdoria eventually ran out winners by just the one goal, but you couldn't fault Genoa's effort. You could say that this game was a victory for fans against commercialism because modern football doesn't take tradition into account. TV companies provide a lot of money but they are killing the atmosphere at certain games with crazy kick-off times.

As I walked back to the hotel with the beaming lights from the stadium in the background, I was glad I'd stayed the extra night to experience this 'derby of the lantern'. The lantern is a major landmark of Genoa with it being a port. Some people wouldn't have this game as a major bucket-list derby, but it puts some of the more glamorous games in the shade. A longer weekend than I expected but a good one.

Hamburg

Hamburg SV v FC St Pauli
(February 6th 2011)

Top tips for Hamburg
Always check to see if a team have ripped up their pitch a few days before a game.
Don't fall asleep in Burger King.
Don't have arguments with robocop police.
Drink sensibly.
Learn the German for gas station.

'Scheiss St Pauli, scheiss St Pauli, scheiss St Pauli' (Shit St Pauli) was being roared down a street just off the Reeperbahn. There's over a hundred Hamburg lads heading down to the Jolly Roger bar, which is a well-known meeting place for St Pauli fans, and they don't look too happy. Windows are getting smashed and a car is getting turned over. Now the police are getting nervous and trying to block the street off. Welcome to Hamburg.

This was one game I was eager to see once the fixture lists had been produced. I'm going to cut to the chase here: Hamburg have a good friendship with Rangers, and St Pauli have a relationship with Celtic. This was the reason why a few pals and I were eager to come over for this game. St Pauli had been promoted and would be playing this fixture for the first time in years.

They did play at St Pauli's Millerntor stadium in September in a one-each draw but, with tickets being very limited, we were all set for the Imtech Arena (as it was then called) in February. These games don't come around very often, and I was pretty sure St Pauli wouldn't be playing in the Bundesliga for a long time.

Flights were pretty cheap. We would fly to Gatwick on Friday evening and get the early flight on Saturday to Hamburg, with the game scheduled for Sunday afternoon. A few weeks before we were due to fly out, there was a spanner thrown in the works when Rangers were drawn to play Celtic in the Scottish Cup at Ibrox. This was on the same weekend as the Hamburg derby. A couple of lads pulled out of the trip but I was adamant that I'd still be going to Germany.

Our hotel was at the top end of the Reeperbahn, right in the heart of the St Pauli district. This was my first time in Hamburg but it was clear when we arrived that quite a few people hadn't been to bed from Friday night. I'd heard all the stories about this infamous area and it's definitely an experience.

We had all sourced match tickets from a very good contact back in Scotland called 'H', so there was no hassle for a change and we could enjoy a full day and night on the piss. What could possibly go wrong?

We'd done a bit of a crawl in various bars and ended up mid afternoon in the Tankstelle Sports Bar. There were quite a few different groups from the UK that had also come over for the game. Rangers, Linfield, Hearts and West Ham were all represented. Everyone seemed to be in good spirits; a few of us enjoyed the spirits too much and I felt pissed by about 6pm.

We were headed back to our hotel to get changed when our taxi driver informed us that the game had been called off due to a waterlogged pitch. At first I thought he was winding us up, but the TV at the hotel confirmed this. Hamburg had decided to rip up their pitch at the start of the week, which under normal circumstances would have been fine. However, due to there being constant rain for most of the week, the pitch couldn't bed in properly. How the fuck this was allowed to happen is a total joke. It was the only major game called off in Germany that weekend.

A couple of my pals were looking at flights to see if they could get back for the Old Firm game the following day, but there was no chance of that with it being an early kick-off. We just had to take it on the chin and enjoy a nice peaceful Saturday night, ha ha.

Once people found out about the game being off, my phone was vibrating with text messages from lads back home taking the piss. To be honest, if the roles were reversed, I'd have been doing the same.

A lot of Hamburg lads were hanging about the Reeperbahn and you could sense something was going to happen. It was getting lively when the group all headed to the Jolly Roger pub. The police were also ready and some teargas was fired. When the police started charging at anything that moved, I immediately jumped in a taxi and shouted 'Tankstelle' to the driver.

I could hear sirens all around but, after a short ride in the taxi, we were sitting at a gas station. I didn't have a clue what was going on, but I didn't need any petrol. I was looking for the Tankstelle Sports Bar. After a few frowns from the driver, I got out and walked to the bar, but was still unsure why we were at the gas station. It turns out, that the German for a gas station is *tankstelle*.

Virtually every entrance and exit to the red-light district had robocops all lined up. The Hamburg lads were growing in numbers all the time. Trying to get in to some bars was proving difficult with the police being very difficult. I started arguing with an officer, which wasn't my wisest move. We eventually all met up in the London Pub and had a good night before splitting up and ending up in different late bars.

Falling asleep in Burger King at 4am wasn't part of my plans but I was rescued by two pals who were passing by, which they are always quick to remind me about.

We all surfaced the next day and watched the Old Firm game in the London Pub. I had a stinking hangover and it was now sinking in about the derby being called off. The whole area was dead on the Sunday and it was a bit of anticlimax, to be honest. The game was arranged for midweek over a week later, so there was no way we were coming back for that. We all said we'd come back the next season for the fixture but St Pauli got relegated, despite winning the rearranged fixture by one goal.

Would I ever get the chance to attend the Hamburg derby?

Glasgow

Celtic v Rangers
(November 12th 1988)
'Old Firm'

Celtic:
Bonner, Morris, Rogan, Aitken, McCarthy, Whyte, Stark, McStay, McAvennie, McGhee, Burns

Rangers:
Woods, Stevens, Brown, Gough, Wilkins, Butcher, Drinkell, I Ferguson, D Ferguson, Cooper, Walters

Ten years of age and I'm going to watch my first Old Firm game at Parkhead at a time when health and safety wasn't heard of. They do say that nothing can prepare you for this fixture – they're fucking right.

I had already been to a few other Rangers' games at this stage, but I'd tried to get to an earlier Old Firm game and failed in my quest. New Year's Day 1988, my dad told me during the day to get a good sleep as we would be hitchhiking very early the following day to Glasgow. There were no trains on New Year's Day and hitchhiking was pretty normal back then.

I could hardly sleep with the excitement. Standing on a slip road with my thumb out at Spaghetti Junction in Birmingham wasn't how I'd imagined the start of my journey to an Old Firm game. My father, uncle and I stood there for two hours, trying to thumb a lift with no success and aborted the mission. I was totally gutted, not just because Rangers lost to two Frank McAvennie goals but because I'd promised my pal I would get him a programme.

After that experience, I wasn't taking anything for granted. This time we were going by train, but we still had the small problem of trying to obtain gold-dust briefs.

We travelled on the Thursday afternoon and stayed with family in Shettleston, in the east end of the city. On the day before the game, we went to watch Rangers train at the Albion training ground, just over the road from Ibrox Stadium. The plan was to talk to the players as they were walking back to Ibrox and hope they might be able to get us some tickets. We were four tickets short, but also knew of other lads from Birmingham that were coming up ticketless. My uncle told the Rangers' player Scott Nesbitt that he and I were ticketless, and he walked us over to the ticket office and got the lady there to give us two briefs. That was a great touch by him, in all honesty.

Finally I could relax in the knowledge that I was going to my first ever Old Firm game. We were still tickets short, though, so anything could happen. I stayed in with my dad on the Friday evening and watched the sports previews talking about the following day's game. All the other lads were out getting pissed. Rangers had won the first Old Firm game of this season 5–1 and were heavy favourites, but Celtic were reigning champions in their centenary year.

On Saturday morning, I felt as nervous as my ten-year-old self could be. Everybody had been telling me for ages that I'd never see anything or hear anything like this derby. My father was still trying to get briefs for the other lads and came back from a pub in Duke Street with some forged tickets. The tickets were exactly the same, apart from a small hologram.

I'm not glorifying people gaining illegal entry but it was the 1980s and attitudes were different then. Rangers were officially allocated 18,000 terracing behind the goal, plus a quarter of the main stand. There was definitely more than that packed in behind the goal. Turnstile operators also never minded getting a little tickle either. In the late eighties Parkhead wasn't exactly a state-of-the-art stadium.

I did what most lads of my era have done and stood outside the pub, waiting for my dad and family to come out and go to the game. It was strictly no children allowed. I was wearing my new gleaming Umbro tracksuit and couldn't have been happier.

When my dad came out and we got a taxi for the short journey, the adrenalin started to kick in. We jumped out of the taxi into a sea of red, white and blue heading down Springfield Road from Parkhead Cross, it was bedlam and also frightening for a ten year old. Our tickets were for the Janefield Street section and as we got the nearer the turnstiles I was shitting myself. This might have been something to do with having a police horse's head right on top of me.

Once we were in, my dad took me straight down to the front behind the goal as it was a bit safer down there. I'd been told stories that in the seventies people standing there used to wear hard hats; this was because bottles used to get thrown from the back and hit the poor fans at the bottom. After an Old Firm Cup Final riot in 1980, all drinking was banned at all stadiums in Scotland.

The noise was unreal and the teams were not even out yet. It seemed like people wanted to get in early to get a few things off their chests. To my right-hand side was the infamous jungle terracing. It did look crazy in there. All around the ground, colours were displayed.

When the teams came out, it went to a different level. The crowds were surging down the terracing. The atmosphere was sheer hatred, which is what makes this derby unique. I had one eye on the game and one eye on the madness around me. Rangers were awarded an early penalty after McCarthy handled in the box. When Mark Walters scored, the place went berserk. It's a hard feeling to describe.

Before I knew much about it, Celtic had scored three goals in quick succession through Butcher (OG), McGhee and Stark – and it wasn't even half-time. Almost three sides of the ground were going crazy. There are not many games in the whole world that can deliver the amount of passion on show here.

If I'm being truthful, I stood in a daze watching that second half and kept staring at the crowd. The game completely passed me by; by all accounts, Celtic ran out worthy 3–1 winners. Most junkies can probably remember their first hit from drugs; well, that was my first hit and I wanted more. Despite the result, I was hooked.

We got the train straight to Birmingham from Central Station after the game. It wasn't a great journey after a defeat but I had a few stories to tell at school on Monday morning.

I feel like we're in a film; fast forward over thirty years and here we are. The world's changed but Rangers still play Celtic and the songs are still the same. In my honest opinion, this game is still up there with the best in the world. Boca v River was on a par for me. Other people may disagree, but don't write this derby off. In certain seasons they can play each other six times and that is without any replays. Could many other big games around the world keep the intensity with that number of games played in a season?

As usual, these days you always get the politically-correct brigade saying how wrong it is that these big bad football fans sing naughty songs. Is that the worst problem we have in society these days? People don't watch this game worldwide for the quality and technical touches, they watch it for the raw passion and want to see tackles flying in. The unique selling point of this game is religion, atmosphere and mayhem. Yes, some of the songs are offensive, but is there a derby in the world without offensive songs? People who sing IRA and UVF songs are not walking around with bombs in their pockets. The day after a game, a lot of people are working alongside each other sharing banter.

I have family in Canada that set their alarms for five in the morning just to watch this fixture down at their local supporters' club. After being to so many of these games, sometimes you take them for granted. I had some friends up from England for a game a few seasons back, which ended in a draw at Parkhead. The looks on their faces when they came out the ground showed me that this fixture has still got it.

I've experienced the highs of winning the league at Parkhead, which I don't think I'll ever beat. That was the day the word 'mayhem' was invented. Pitch invasions, the referee getting struck by a coin and a fan falling from the top tier of a stand. I have also seen a last-minute cup-final winner. I've experienced painful drubbings from Celtic, which you have to take on the chin. I cried my eyes out at the 1989 Scottish Cup Final when Celtic won 1–0. I've experienced an Old Firm game with no away fans in April 1994. That was a terrible game and a terrible atmosphere.

At the moment, both away supporters allocations have been cut to around 800 tickets. I don't know how this will end up long term. I'm sitting on the fence, to be honest, as I can see both sides of the argument ,although I hope it doesn't get to the stage where there isn't a single away fan in the stadium.

Some people say that this game has been diluted over the years. The days of a 3pm kick-off on a Saturday afternoon are well and truly gone, unless there is a cup final. The authorities, police and TV companies now have the fixture permanently played at midday.

You could say that there is very little trouble at the grounds these days, but that doesn't tell the full story. People are out drinking earlier before a game and most hospitals in the west of Scotland and beyond, let alone the police cells, can be at breaking point on a match day.

The west of Scotland isn't as black and white as people think. There are lots of mixed marriages now and people have moved on. I work and play football in Glasgow with Celtic fans and generally get on with them. On an Old Firm day, though, I wouldn't mix with any of them. I like to be with my own company and I'm sure they're the same.

Both clubs now rely on promoting playing European football and the Old Firm game when trying to sign players. Celtic got to a European final in 2003, and Rangers did the same in 2008, but that would be hard to do again. In the current format, the days of being able to compete financially with English clubs are over. Clubs such as Bournemouth can trump any wages on offer at both Scottish clubs so two clubs with big histories in the game are in limbo.

I do think people should be proud of this game rather than hiding behind the curtains. When we were in South America, we had Brazilians telling us that they would love to attend this fixture. It still has appeal and is definitely one game where fans don't take selfies with opposing players. Some derbies are purely about football. This derby has it all, with religion, politics and two very big teams in the same city.

I could write a whole book on aspects of this derby but I won't bore you with all the details. There might not be a Gascoigne, Laudrup, Larsson, Di Canio, De Boer or Van Hooijdonk anymore, but this game still makes the hairs on the back of your neck stand up.

MILAN

Inter v Milan
(February 27th 2005)
'Derby della Madonnina'

Top tips for Milan
Always wear sunglasses, even when it's freezing.
Don't be jealous of people draped in expensive clobber.
Wear at least two pairs of socks to a game in February.
Don't think you're the next James Richardson, with a massive ice cream and a *La Gazzetta dello Sport* newspaper.

I was born in 1978, but my first real World Cup that I watched from start to finish was Italia 90. You could not help but look in awe at some of the stadiums. Grounds in the UK at that time were falling apart. From seeing top-flight games being played at Plough Lane in England, we were seeing the San Siro and Stadio Olimpico. The stadiums looked massive and I couldn't wait to sample them once I was older.

Most people growing up in that era were glued to Channel Four's coverage of *Gazzetta Italia*. The sight of James Richardson with a gigantic ice cream or coffee and a pile of newspapers next to him was great Saturday morning viewing.

At the time Serie A was by far the best league in the world; all the best players played there. Milan had Baresi, Gullit, Rijkaard, Van Basten, to name but a few. Inter had their share of famous names as well, with Matthäus, Klinsmann, Brehme, Zenga and many more. It really was exciting times football-wise in Italy. The Derby della Madonnina was always one I watched and dreamed of going to. It's called this because there is a Virgin Mary statue on top of the Duomo cathedral and is often referred to as 'Little Madonna'.

Milan is a very cosmopolitan city and I immediately think of designer clothing, great food and the Giuseppe Meazza Stadium when the city is mentioned. I was still living in Birmingham at this time, so travelling to Milan was very easy compared to some places, a direct flight to Malpensa airport on the Saturday morning with my partner. The game was being played on the Sunday evening.

The centre of Milan is very much what you'd expect of a stylish city, but the outskirts looks really run down with graffiti everywhere. Piazza del Duomo is where most tourists flock to. The cathedral does look pretty impressive and the area around these streets, with all the designer boutiques, is very smart. The Galleria Vittorio Emanuele II shopping mall is a work of art in itself. The Italians know how to dress but everybody seemed to be wearing sunglasses in February. You can also see people wearing Armani head to toe yet see poor people only a few yards away.

I was very lazy in looking for match tickets on this trip. I'd had a quick browse online but it wasn't exactly easy, and at this particular time I didn't always have internet access. My plan was to walk up to the ground, get tickets outside from one of the many touts and get the best price. If I was going to this derby now, I would do things completely differently. In 2005 you didn't need ID and names on the tickets; it was pretty straightforward.

Milan has a very vibrant restaurant scene but it's not exactly overloaded with bars. There's a few Irish ones kicking about, but the Saturday evening was spent in a trattoria and a couple of cocktail bars.

After seeing a few of the sights on Sunday morning, I was ready for a few beers and to start sampling some of this derby atmosphere. We got the metro to Lotto station, which is a good twenty-minute walk to the stadium. My plan was to come out of the station and haggle over the price of tickets, but we were well early and there weren't many people around. I must have had a tourist sign on my head because, when we were heading to the stadium, some touts approached us and told us in broken English that 'these tickets were like gold dust'. After putting on my best poker face and telling them I wasn't too fussed about going the game, we paid €20 over the face-value amount. All things considered, it wasn't the worst deal in the world and we now had three hours before kick-off to get pissed on some Chianti.

Making our way to a nearby bar, I noticed that all the scarf/flag/badge sellers were selling items for both Inter and AC. Upon arriving at the bar, it had both sets of supporters. This match between the Nerazzurri (black/blue) and the Rossoneri (red/black) has worldwide appeal and doesn't have any political or religious connections. I'm not going to lie, I was a bit disappointed seeing everybody mixing in the bar. I much prefer derby games to have a bit of needle in them, I suppose you could say it's similar to Liverpool v Everton. Having said that, these two sets of supporters are very passionate about their teams.

The Giuseppe Meazza Stadium (San Siro) is very impressive from outside. Yes, the facilities aren't great inside but as you catch sight of it for the first time it's definitely a fantastic sight. I would say that it's one of the best stadiums I've seen from the outside. The Nou Camp doesn't look that big from outside because the pitch is under ground level, but that isn't the case here. The spiral staircases look great and add to the spectacle. It can be seen from a great distance and is very imposing. I know that they close tiers for games when the crowd is small, but it's always full and vibrant when this derby is on.

Our tickets were for the East Stand but at the corner of the Curva Nord, which is where the Inter Ultras are situated. Technically this was Inters home game. The Curva Sud housed all the Milan fans while the other two stands were fairly mixed. The Ultras from both clubs had been in very early and the tifo displays from both ends were different class. The only problem with the Inter display was that it didn't stay up for long and slid down to the front, much to the amusement of the Milan fans. I'm not sure what the Italian is for 'what the fucking hell was that?' but that's what we would have been singing in the UK.

The atmosphere was very loud, with loads of firecrackers going off as you'd expect. The players emerged to sheer bedlam and, once the game started, it was frantic. The quality of the players in this match was of an unbelievable standard. In fact, I'm going to list these teams before I go any further so you get a clearer picture of the quality.

INTER: Toldo, J. Zanetti, Cordoba, Mihajlovic, Favalli, C. Zanetti, Cambiasso, Stankovic, Veron, Vieri, Martins. SUBS: Emre, Adriano, Van der Meyde

MILAN: Dida, Cafu, Nesta, Maldini, Kaladze, Gattuso, Pirlo, Seedorf, Kakà, Rui Costa, Crespo. SUBS: Costacurta, Serginho, Ambrosini

There weren't a lot of chances but Inter looked on top for most of the game. Nesta and Maldini, two of the best defenders in the world, weren't going to let anyone run away and score an easy goal. The Ultras kept the atmosphere very loud but it never felt intimidating.

My feet were numb with the cold, and a guy coming round selling miniature drinks was my man of the match. In saying that, watching Gattuso running about like a Tasmanian devil made me feel warm too. With all the quality on the pitch, I couldn't believe it could end up goalless. With fifteen minutes to go, Kaka turned in a Gattuso shot for the only goal of the game. The Milan end was bouncing, and it took quite a while for the smoke to lift from the goal celebrations.

Although I had no preference who won, I felt bad for the Inter fans next to me as they had given their all in a derby and had nothing to show for it. The first hour or so after getting beaten by your rivals is torture, as many of you know.

On leaving the stadium and walking back to Lotto metro, it felt like virtually every person must have come on a scooter as they were everywhere.

We could tell who the waiters supported back in the centre by the look on their faces. I do love how they talk with their hands going everywhere, but no one can deny how passionate they are about football.

At the time of writing, Italian football is slowly getting its reputation back after years of scandal and a drop in standards. A few months after attending this fixture, Milan were 3–0 up at half-time in the Champions League Final. We all know what happened after that.

It was a good experience and a real football atmosphere, although it did feel strange with a lot of fans sitting almost side by side. This was my first Italian derby and was definitely one to tick off the list. The history of this game and the size of the two clubs means that it will always be up there when it comes to derbies.

Dublin

Republic Of Ireland v Northern Ireland
(November 15th 2018)

Top tips for Dublin
Try and get an earlier flight.
Enjoy the city.
Tell your pal to change his ringtone.
Temple Bar area is as expensive as you'd expect.

Out of all the games I've been to, I think it's fair to say that this one has a long political history. At the moment, with the Brexit situation, there was a potential for a bit of trouble. This game was only a friendly but both countries have history, as we all know.

I remember the game in 1993 in Belfast, when Ireland secured a draw to qualify for the 1994 World Cup in the USA. It was a very hostile atmosphere and at that time the Troubles were still ongoing. There's been a lot of water under the bridge since then though; the peace deal is still standing to this day and will hopefully continue.

My friend Mikey from Belfast had mentioned about going to this fixture, but with it being a friendly I wasn't too fussed. The more thought I gave it though, the more I wanted to go. The teams don't play that often and the last fixture was played in 2011. Both teams are not exactly in a golden era either, but have managed to qualify for some recent tournaments. There's still a fierce rivalry and, when you throw in the history, then it's a definite thumbs-up from me.

I was planning on a little weekend break to London with the Mrs, but train prices were a bit silly when I looked at booking. Mikey had called me and assured me we would get match tickets for the Northern Ireland section if we fancied it. After a quick check for the flights, the trip became a lot clearer. We could fly on Thursday afternoon from Glasgow to Dublin at 3pm with Ryanair for less than a tenner. We could then fly on Friday afternoon from Dublin to London, and back to Glasgow on Sunday at a decent price. I get the football and we get a weekend in London for Xmas shopping and the theatre. Everybody wins.

With all the history between these two countries, it's funny to think how there is only one rugby team between them. Players from both countries join up as one to play rugby. Even when the conflict was at its worst, this was still the case. A few weeks before this fixture, I watched an excellent documentary on BT Sport about the Ireland rugby team. It showed all the difficulties and cultural differences between them.

I'd never been to Dublin before and all I ever heard is how expensive it is for a drink. When I was growing up it seemed to be that nearly all stag and hen weekends were in Dublin, but not so much now. I was planning on going there in 1998 to watch Rangers play Shelbourne, but UEFA stepped in and moved the fixture to Tranmere in England. This was at the height of the marching season and it was probably a sensible move.

Getting tickets for this fixture wasn't as smooth as I thought it would be. It was fairly straightforward to get tickets for the Ireland section, but with Northern Ireland only getting a small allocation it was quite strict. I thought we would get to our hotel and then meet my friends for a few drinks and head to the game. After registering through a supporters' club, we were told that everybody had to pick up their tickets at a venue around a mile away from the Aviva Stadium. This wasn't ideal as our flight was landing at 4pm – if it was on time.

We landed around half four but once we had cleared passport control, it was just after five o'clock. At the height of rush hour on an airport bus to the city centre, time was very tight. The only thing in our favour was that we were staying in the Leeson Bridge area of the city and the bus stopped outside our hotel. It was only just over a mile to the Aviva Stadium from there.

I was surprised to see so many tourists in Dublin on a dark night in November, and my first impressions of the city were good. By the time we checked in and threw our bags in the room, there was just over an hour till kick-off but we still had to pick up our match tickets.

Mikey and Cubby were staying around the corner from our hotel so we quickly met up with them and ordered a taxi to the pick-up point. Our taxi driver arrived and I could sense he was a bit of a character. He had a picture of Jesus and rosary beads hanging in the cab. When we told him where we needed to go, he looked a bit puzzled. He said, 'There's fuck all up there, it's an industrial estate.'

Whilst he was explaining this, Cubby's phone started ringing with 'The Sash My Father Wore' as his ringtone. This is a well-known loyalist song and the penny dropped with the taxi driver that we were picking up Northern Ireland tickets. He had a good laugh with us, to be fair, but did say, 'Of all the fucking groups I had to pick up...'

It turned out that the pick-up point was a GAA club and, surprisingly, the ticket pick up was smooth. If I'm being honest, I think this was way over the top for a friendly.

With the imposing stadium in the distance, it was now a quick walk to try and make the kick-off. There was no real segregation on the approach to the Aviva and I wasn't too concerned as most people were mingling with no issues. As we crossed the road, I could hear 'Fuck yer Union Jack, we want our country back' being sung by a few dafties, but most people just ignored it. That could have turned out differently though, if there'd been a bigger crowd nearby. After a body search on the way in we just got to our seats as the teams came out.

As the band started to play 'God Save the Queen' a lot of the stadium started to boo and whistle to drown out the anthem. The Norn Iron fans, as they are known, then returned the favour to drown out 'Amhran na bhFiann' (Soldier's Song). Although this was a friendly, it definitely wasn't in the stands. A few songs were sung from both sides that weren't exactly from *Songs of Praise*.

In the small section that we were in, it was clear that a lot of people had been enjoying a few drinks prior to this game. We were behind the goal and had a great view of the pitch. I wasn't too impressed with the concourse area below us, as it was very small and cramped.

The game started well but both sides cancelled out each other for large periods of the first half and it was a bit flat. James McLean constantly got booed with every touch; his manager Martin O'Neill had admitted that if this game had been played in Belfast, he wouldn't have played him. This is due to his annual refusal to wear a poppy on his shirt and he'd also switched allegiance to Ireland.

This is by no means a great Ireland team: the glory days of Keane, McGrath, Houghton, Aldridge, Staunton and Quinn are long gone. Norn Iron started to take control of the game and should have won with the chances they missed. Jones was the biggest culprit, missing a one on one. If it hadn't been for Darren Randolph in goal, it might have been a comfortable victory. Steven Davis looked like he was playing with slippers on in the second half.

The attendance was just over 31,000 in a stadium with a capacity of 51,000. I'm not sure whether this was due to the stupid pricing for a friendly or the general apathy towards the home team.

Once the full-time whistle blew, the Norn Iron fans were kept in for around twenty minutes. They sang 'We're On Our Way' for the full duration. There were a few scuffles with stewards as people wanted to get out, but it was handbag stuff really.

While we were waiting to get out, they were already starting to put the rugby posts up at the far end for Saturday's game against New Zealand. When they built this shiny new stadium in 2010, I don't think they paid too much attention to the away section. It was very narrow and tight when trying to get out until you could get to the corner.

We started making our way to the city centre and everything was relatively calm. We stopped off at the Grand Canal area in a trendy restaurant bar. It was €7 for a pint but it was warm and relaxing in the bar. Most people in there had no interest in the match that had just been played and were quite friendly. I could have stayed in this bar all night but one of the terms of this trip was a night in the Temple Bar area with the Mrs.

As most of you probably know, Temple Bar is an area full of bars playing live music and tourists. As it was my first time in the city, it was one of those things to tick off the list. Even though it was Thursday night, it was still very busy. Let's be honest, though, it is totally overpriced.

After going to a few of these bars, we called it a night around half two. It had been a long day considering I'd done half a shift at work with a half seven start in the morning, before going the airport.

Although this was literally a flying visit, the few parts of Dublin I saw were decent. The locals I met were good people, too. Maybe people have moved away from all the bitterness and hatred. I can't help but think that if this game had been a World Cup qualifier, it would have been a lot more intense, and maybe there would have been a lot more hatred from both sides.

I may head back here again one day. It was another football rivalry ticked off the list and, before you ask, no, I didn't try a Guinness.

Rotterdam

Feyenoord v Ajax
(January 27th 2019)
'De Klassieker'

Top tips for Rotterdam
Be prepared to have pints thrown over you.
Never say Robin van Persie is past it.
Always have faith in football.
When at a rave, you need to bounce.

It's December 2009, and there's a power cut in my street in Glasgow. There's been no power for around an hour when somebody starts banging my front door. As I make my way to the door, I can make out the outline of a big guy. My first thoughts are that he is coming to burgle my flat and he's just checking to see if anybody is in. I open the door quickly with a metal vase in my hand and ask him, 'What the fuck do you want?'

He asks about the power in a strange accent and whether I have any spare candles.

After a few questions, I invite him in to my flat to give him the candles. He is staying one flat below me and explains that he's from Rotterdam, working in Glasgow, and his name is Dennis. He sees a Rangers' picture on my table and says he knows a lad called Adds who follows Rangers, who just happens to be my friend as well. It's a small world and all that.

I must have been feeling happy that day as I even offered him a few bottles of beer. I tell him that I've been to Ajax, AZ Alkmaar and Feyenoord whilst following Rangers, but would never, ever go back to Rotterdam. He tells me he's a Feyenoord fan and has been a season-ticket holder. Ten years later, and it's through Dennis that I get a ticket for Feyenoord v Ajax.

I'd phoned my mate Adds just before Xmas and asked him what games he had planned for 2019 and he'd mentioned this fixture at the end of January. The flights were fairly cheap and it would only be one night away; I'd worry about accommodation once Xmas was out the way.

I vowed never to return to Rotterdam when I was there in February 2002. I was there to see Rangers in a UEFA Cup tie and arrived ticketless with some friends a few hours before kick-off. I'd heard all the stories about how mad the Feyenoords firm was, but I didn't give a fuck back then.

A lot of ticketless Rangers' fans stayed back in Amsterdam but we went through to Rotterdam. Once off the train at the De Kuip stadium, we were hassled straight away. It was still early but there were different groups congregating already. There's a tunnel from the train station straight to the away-section turnstiles. This was no use to us, as we were hunting for tickets.

After seeing a few people getting attacked and the police being less than friendly, we were told in certain terms to 'fuck off back to Amsterdam'. It was moody as fuck. The police couldn't even guarantee our safety at the main train station, and told us to walk to one about half a mile away. Anyway, we were back in the Dam for kick-off and heard a few horror stories of Rangers being in the home sections and getting attacked big time. My attitude at that time was fuck Rotterdam.

Over time, my attitude towards Rotterdam relaxed. Through Dennis, I have met some great Feyenoord lads over the years who have came over to Glasgow for Old Firm games. They have always told me to come over for De Klassieker.

The big problem with this fixture is the ban on away fans. It's now eleven years since they were allowed to visit each other's stadium. It got too much hassle for the authorities, with people pulling cords on trains to get off and cause trouble. It's a shame because I believe every big rivalry game needs away fans. You need to noise each other up. After speaking to the Feyenoord lads, they all agreed that the fixture isn't the same without the away fans.

Like most people in January, I was skint. I'd been paid before Xmas and wasn't getting my next wage until four days after the fixture. I did think about pulling out of this trip but I'm now glad that I stuck to my guns and went. There were a few other things on in Rotterdam that weekend and hotel prices were quite expensive. I eventually managed to book cheap accommodation in a very handy spot, and was literally in the room for five hours.

Adds and Dennis were flying out at ten on Saturday morning and I was flying from Glasgow at half five in the evening. I knew I'd be playing catch up when I got there as they were going to be bang on the booze all day. When I landed at Schiphol airport, I turned my phone on to find over one hundred Whatsapp messages. Virtually all the messages and video clips were about the trouble that had happened earlier in the day at Millwall v Everton in the FA Cup.

After getting the express train into Rotterdam, I navigated my way to my hotel. What the fuck did people do before Google maps? After throwing my very small bag in the room, I went to meet the lads in the Panenka sports bar. There were some good faces in this bar and it's fair to say Adds and Dennis had enjoyed a good drink already. I was introduced to some people for the first time who were great company. After a few more bars in the cool district, and a few Belgian strong beers, we settled for the night in a bar playing old-school dance tunes.

The next morning I took a stroll along the Erasmusbrug bridge to go and get Adds and Dennis out of their beds. While walking along this bridge, I could see the developing skyline of Rotterdam's financial district. It's a much better city now than I saw for a few short hours in 2002.

Considering there's only an hour between the two cities, Amsterdam and Rotterdam are completely different. Excuse the stereotypes, but Rotterdam is a working city, although I don't think much work got done the day after this game. There are other teams in Rotterdam, so technically this isn't a derby but this is the biggest game for the two clubs.

After getting a breakfast where you virtually had to do everything yourself except cook the fucking thing, we headed on the tram to meet up with the Feyenoord lads at Cafe De Oude Sluis. Just like in Germany, the public transport is free for a few hours before and after kick-off for fans travelling to and from the game. Why can't we do this in the UK?

The café-type bar was buzzing already. A few people looked a bit rough from the night before but you could feel the atmosphere building. There were a few bits of Feyenoord memorabilia on the walls and it was mobbed by 11am. Everybody seemed to be buying jugs of beer, which is a great idea. You buy a big jug for around €17 and they give you a load of plastic glasses to dish out. It saves big queues at the bar on a match day.

My mate Scott was here with his girlfriend. He's a West Bromwich Albion fan and has knew the Feyenoord lads for a few years. His accent is pathetic but he's a great lad. While he went the toilet, me and Adds did the thing that lads do on a wind up and asked his girlfriend why they weren't married yet. She agreed with us, so we told all the lads that Scott was getting married soon and we had a stag weekend to get sorted. When he came out of the toilet, all the lads congratulated him and he didn't have a clue what was going on. He did call me a cunt after that, though.

It was pissing down and freezing outside and I was debating with myself whether to stay in the warm pub or go to the game. We'd all had a good drink but we walked the ten minutes to De Kuip stadium. The two Marcos had given me and Adds two season tickets to use and wouldn't take a penny off us.

The walk to the stadium brought a few painful flashbacks from 2002 to me. One thing I did notice was the general apathy amongst the Feyenoord supporters outside the ground. This is their main game and always will be, yet people were predicting a three or four goal victory to Ajax.

Our seats were at the corner flag on the same side as the dugouts. Giovanni Van Bronckhorst had announced a few days before that he would be leaving Feyenoord at the end of the current season and he got a great reception.

Despite no away fans, it was a loud atmosphere to start with. After eight minutes Schone put a free kick in the top corner to put Ajax one up. Maybe the lads were right, this was going to be an easy win for Ajax. My first thought was to head back to the pub and get back on the booze but, out of respect for Marco, I decided to stay till half-time. Out of nowhere, Feyenoord equalised through Toornstra and then went ahead with a goal from Berghuis. It was bouncing.

I went down to the toilet and then tried to get a few beers, but you could only pay in tokens which you had to get outside before the game. I got back to my seat and Adds told me it was now two each, as Ajax had equalised through Ziyech. With no away fans, I would never have known a thing. I did say that when the teams started this game that Robin van Persie was well past his best, but he scored two good goals either side of half-time to ram those words down my throat.

I decided to stay at half-time as I was actually enjoying the game and the atmosphere. Unlike in England, you can take your beers to your seats and watch the game. This caused me a problem, though, as it's like being at a concert where everybody just starts chucking their half-full plastic glasses forward.

So, covered in drink, I witnessed Feyenoord score two more goals through Vilhena and Ayoub to comfortably win this match 6–2. Even with ten minutes to go, the fans around me were still nervous which I couldn't understand. At that point they were three goals in front, yet were sitting biting their nails. If that was an Old Firm game, the place would have been rocking.

Once the full-time whistle went, the players did a lap of honour. The tannoy system started playing techno tunes that everyone – and I mean everyone – was bouncing in tune to. That was good to see. We then walked back to the same pub with everybody in high spirits despite the ice-cold rain and wind.

I did feel like a bit of a fraud for a short while after in the pub, as people were hugging each other; you could see how much this victory meant to them. A few of the lads were saying I now had to come back every year for this fixture as a good-luck charm. I'm sure my Mrs will love that.

Marco told me that in over thirty years of being a season-ticket holder, he had only seen four victories over Ajax at De Kuip. Here's this football tourist like me just rocking up for the first time and witnessing a victory of that margin.

After quite a few more jugs of beer, we left the lads in good spirits and made our way to Schiphol Airport. Part of me was left wondering how good the atmosphere would have been if the Ajax fans had been there. Another weird thing I couldn't get my head around was that some Feyenoord songs were sung in Dutch and some in English. Who decides?

This was literally a mad twenty-four hours and we were back in Glasgow for half ten. I really enjoyed the experience and made some new friends.

Feyenoord 6   **Ajax 2**

Toornstra (16')   **Schone (8')**
Berghuis (31')   **Ziyech (33')**
van Persie (42', 56')
Vilhena (75')
Ayoub (84')

Lisbon

Sporting v Benfica
(May 5th 2018)
'Derby de Lisboa'

Top tips for Lisbon
Wait until the last minute for tickets.
Don't think you are eighteen again in nightclubs at 6am.
Enjoy one of the best cities around.
Be prepared to be offered drugs everywhere.

This city has to be one of the most underrated in my opinion. It has a great nightlife, beaches not far away and a decent climate for most of the year. I'm not a travel expert, but Lisbon ticks a lot of boxes for a long weekend away. If you throw in a derby between two very big clubs then you're on to a winner; even my Mrs gave it the thumbs up.

I'd visited this city in March for the first time and was well impressed, so when the chance came up for a weekend away in May I jumped at it. Like most of these trips, the football games abroad tend to get moved for TV, sometimes with only a week's notice. This can be a pain in the arse when booking flights and hotels, so I thought I'd play safe with this trip. We booked to fly out from Glasgow to Lisbon on the Thursday, and then get a train to Albufeira on the Monday morning and stay there for two nights to make it into a holiday. It got the approval from the Mrs. If the game got moved I was covered with the four nights in Lisbon.

I wasn't overly concerned about getting match tickets for this fixture, as I thought it wouldn't be too much of an issue. As the week got nearer, I could see that Porto, Sporting and Benfica were all at the top of the table with virtually nothing separating them. Benfica had won the league for the past four seasons and were favourites again. The derby would be the penultimate game of the season and could decide the title. That's when I knew it would be tight for tickets. I even chanced my luck and sent a message to the woman who was renting us her apartment for tickets, but she had no joy in getting any.

With a lot of cruise ships coming into Lisbon, it's always busy and lively with tourists. Tourists attract different types of salesmen but I couldn't believe how many times I was offered drugs – and not by your normal drug dealer type of guy, either. Smart people wearing suits were offering you anything you wanted. After a quick search online, it seems Portugal has relaxed their drug laws and crime levels have gone down. To me it seems they are basically saying people doing recreational drugs are okay, but if you're walking about with a hold-all full of drugs you're getting lifted. Is this the right way to do it? It seems to be.

After a decent day and night on Thursday, when I woke up on Friday morning my plan was to head over to Estadio Jose Alvalade and try to get two tickets. If you don't ask, you don't get is my motto. I went alone to the ground and, as my metro was approaching the Campo Grande stop, I could see a very long queue snaking around the stadium. I joined the end of the queue and got talking to a local who spoke good English. He informed me that this queue was for tickets for a cup final that was being played in two weeks' time.

There was one small window with a sign saying Benfica tickets but for members only. I tried my best 'I've come all the way to Lisbon to see this special derby' chat-up line, but it was no good. I was told it was unlikely there would be a public sale. A couple of touts were standing nearby and, after hearing my conversation, they offered me tickets but at way over the odds. The thing is, like in most places, how do you know these tickets are legit?

A normal supporter then offered me a season ticket sitting next to him for face value, I appreciated that but I needed two, as the Mrs wanted to come to the match. Can you imagine my conversation with my partner later in the day, telling her I had one ticket and she could spend Saturday evening on her own?

I caved in and went on to a well-known ticket agency website and purchased two tickets for £100 each. We were to pick them up from a nearby hotel before the game. Everybody has an opinion about these type of ticket agencies, and they are robbing bastards with their extra charges, but it saved a lot of hassle even though I still felt there would be a public sale the following day, as Sporting couldn't win the league due to dropped points. Benfica would need to win the match to have a chance of winning the league in the last game the following weekend. Sporting also needed to win to get a Champions League spot.

With the tickets sorted, we could now relax and we spent a nice day in Belem, which is a great place and about ten minutes on a train. The city was gearing up for the following weekend's Eurovision contest, with lots of stages being set up. After some cracking Portuguese vino, we finished the night off in the Bairro Alto area, which is really lively with loads of bars and a great vibe.

I would have liked to have seen Benfica's Estadio da Luz, but there wasn't enough time. It's only one mile from the Estadio Jose Alvalade and both of these were constructed for the 2004 European Championships. Benfica's stadium is 15,000 bigger, with a capacity of 65,000. They both looked impressive from the outside when we flew over them. These two clubs have given us two of the greatest players to have ever played the game: Ronaldo and Eusebio.

After a quick check online on Saturday morning, there was a public sale and the tickets were between €50 and €70 each. Some you win and some you lose, I suppose. I should have gone with my gut instinct but, hey ho, I'd already got them.

With the game being played on Saturday evening, there was plenty of time for drinking but we took it quite easy during the day. It was touching thirty degrees in the afternoon and for once I was sensible. Most supporters were drinking in the city centre, as the area around the stadium isn't overloaded with bars. I didn't see any Benfica colours before the game but I think they had a march to the stadium. They had only been allocated around 2,500 tickets.

We arrived at the hotel to pick up our tickets from the agency. A big fat guy was sitting like Del Boy with a wad of envelopes containing tickets. There were probably another ten people in front of us, mostly tourists. When booking these tickets, they'd said that if better tickets became available in the stadium they would upgrade us. This was the first time I'd used an agency and I thought that would be a load of bollocks, but our tickets were upgraded at no extra cost.

Being a Rangers' fan, I did find it weird being surrounded by 40,000-plus green-and-white-hooped supporters, although my Mrs did tell me to 'have a day off and fucking grow up'.

There was a shopping centre next to the metro station that had a few bars, which was okay for a quick drink. Our seats were in the upper tier around the halfway line and were cracking. The atmosphere was building and the Ultras had three big banners on display behind the goal. The main banner was an image of Freddie Kruger from the film *Nightmare on Elm Street* chasing Benfica supporters.

It was a very colourful background to this derby, and it felt like everyone in the stadium had a club shirt on. The small band of Benfica fans were well up for it as well. The game started but only for a few seconds, as the Sporting Ultras threw a lot of flares onto the pitch. They were thrown right by their own goalkeeper, which I thought was very strange.

Benfica started really well and hit the post, and I thought there was only going to be one winner at that stage, but Sporting gradually came in to it. I wouldn't say that both teams were loaded with household names, but it was played with a lot of pace and passion. A few fans may have gained access illegally, as there were people sitting in the stairways and asking if there were any empty seats in my row. I didn't sense a lot of hatred from the stands to the opposing players but there was still a good atmosphere.

Considering there was a lot riding on this game, you kind of expected there to be a lot of nerves, and the game was littered with stray passes and a lack of cutting edge. The one player that I wanted to see was the Benfica centre half, Luisao, but he was on the bench.

A bare-chested Sporting fan kept us amused for most of the second half. He was steaming drunk and kept running down the stairs, ranting all the time about anyone and anything. I'd say he could have been a Portuguese version of Rab C. Nesbitt, minus the string vest.

With five minutes remaining, we decided to make a dash to the metro for a quick getaway. The Benfica fans were slowing coming to terms with the fact that the league was slipping away and the game ended in a goalless draw. It wasn't a classic game by any means, but it was still a decent derby. It would have been good to see what the atmosphere was like with a few goals, but the two teams cancelled each other out.

We got off at Marques de Pombal metro stop and saw a lot of Porto fans driving with flags hanging out their windows and tooting their horns. It was their first title since 2013 and, with the derby being a draw, the league was now won.

After a quick change, we headed out for a night of madness. The Bairro Alto area is full of bars that stay open till 3am. After a few drinks there, we went down to Cais do Sodre, which is full of clubs that are open till 6am. My clubbing career has had its best days, but we had done my thing in going to the football and my Mrs wanted to stay out all night. We ended up in a club called Musicbox. It was one of those clubs where everybody is drinking water. I was propped up a wall, still trying to down Superbocks.

At around 6am I staggered in to a taxi, pissed and tired, but all in all it was a good day and a great trip. Get yourself to Lisbon, is my advice.

England v Scotland

(November 17th 1999)
'The world's oldest international match'

England:
Seaman, Southgate, P Neville Campbell, Adams, Beckham, Ince, Redknapp, Scholes, Owen, Shearer

Scotland:
Sullivan, Dailly, Davidson, Hendry, Weir, Burley, Collins, Ferguson, Hutchison, McCann, Dodds

October 1999, and England and Scotland are drawn out the hat to play each other in the European Championship play off over two legs. The tournament is being staged in Belgium and Holland in 2000. You could say there's quite a lot at stake in these games.

In international football there aren't many rivalries that can match this. The teams first locked horns against each other in Glasgow in 1872, making this the world's oldest international football fixture. The last fixture before the play off was a 2–0 victory for England at Wembley during Euro 96. It used to be a regular fixture on the calendar but got stopped in 1989. The police were always moaning about the trouble but, in truth, the fixture was past its sell-by date then and needed a rest.

My dad is Scottish and was forever telling me stories of Wembley weekends and how he never missed a game between the two countries for several years at Wembley or Hampden.

When people of a certain age think of Scotland playing at Wembley, they instantly think of fans swinging on crossbars and a pitch invasion. This fixture used to be massive, and there would be a tartan army invasion every two years. In the mid-eighties, the football casual scene was on the rise. The authorities even got this fixture played midweek in 1986 to try and limit the number of fans travelling down and prevent trouble. I think it's fair to say that at some of these games at Wembley there were more than 50,000

Scottish fans. This play-off game was a completely different era and the official away allocation would be around 8,000.

As I'd never been to this fixture before, I was adamant that I was going to London for a day on the piss and would try to get tickets. My mate Blucky struck gold when he got four briefs through the hotline, which was virtually jammed as soon as the lines opened. We also had our mate Digger studying down in Luton; he had a student flat where we could crash, so we'd thought we'd kill two birds and see him and then head through to London.

The first leg was played at Hampden Park on Saturday 13th, and the second leg was played on Wednesday 17th at Wembley. England won at Hampden with two goals from Paul Scholes in a 2–0 victory. It was a tight game but everybody had written off Scotland for the second leg already. There were reports of trouble in Glasgow, but we weren't expecting any in London.

The plan was to go to Luton on Tuesday evening and stay for two nights, as it's only around forty minutes on the train to Central London from there. I'd just started a new job and could only get one day off work, so I would have to get back to Birmingham after the game and be in work on Thursday.

A night in a student flat on a Tuesday night should be a standard night, right? We ripped the arse out of the drink and decided not to get a wink of sleep, which wasn't the greatest of ideas.

Totally fucked and hungover, we headed into London for opening time after a king-size breakfast. The game was starting at 8pm; it was going to be a long shift on the booze. We started off in the Roundhouse pub in Covent Garden and there were already different little England firms kicking about. With only a few Scotland fans coming down, a few of these England firms were eyeballing each other It was a bit moody, with a fair percentage of Stone Island jackets kicking about. After a bit of a pub crawl, we settled in All Bar One in Leicester Square. Blucky decided to get us a bottle of Moet on his works card after he lost a bet between us. This Wednesday afternoon was turning a bit hazy.

A few days before this game, my brother had phoned and told me to meet up with him in Trafalgar Square during Wednesday afternoon. He said he'd be wearing a 'See-You-Jimmy' wig and I wouldn't be able to miss him. I didn't have a mobile phone at this time in my life, so I couldn't phone him.

For a lot of Scotland fans it's a tradition to go to Trafalgar Square, get pissed with loads of crates of booze and jump into the fountains. It was starting to get dark when Blucky, Digger, Reg and I headed down there. The only slight problem was that every Scotland fan there had a Jimmy wig on. I can also clarify that nobody was in the fountains as it was fucking freezing. So, after having a search for half an hour, we eventually found my brother and went into a boozer next to Charing Cross. At this stage of the day, the pub was bouncing and it was a good laugh.

We headed over to Wembley on the tube. It felt a little bit special when we got off the train and walked down Wembley Way. This would be the last ever England v Scotland match with the famous twin towers, which were due to be bulldozed in the new year. The truth is that this historic stadium was showing its age and needed a transformation.

Our tickets were right next to the Scotland section and we had a decent view. Once the anthems were out the way, the very famous referee Pierluigi Collina got us underway. England started really well and were looking to finish the game off. Gradually Scotland came into it and it wasn't a surprise when they took the lead through Hutchison. Neil McCann had crossed a great ball to the back post and Hutchison out-jumped Adams to score. It was game on!

The second half started and Scotland were starting to pull the strings through Collins and Ferguson. England were getting more nervous as the half wore on. With ten minutes remaining, Dailly had a header saved by Seaman, which would have forced extra time. Digger wasn't too fussed about the game but had planned to be back in Luton for his student club night before the entrance curfew. Scotland just couldn't get the breakthrough and England had scraped through. The game finished England 0, Scotland 1.

It was another glorious failure for the Scotland team, although they could claim a moral victory in the last game under the twin towers. I was on a mission to get to my last train from London Euston, and Digger and the lads made it back in time to Luton for another evening's drinking. Oh yes, I was lovely and fresh in work the next day, too.

Fast forward again and I'm writing this in 2019. Obviously a few things have changed. Digger is no longer a student, a few of us have lost a bit of hair and Blucky is still moaning about buying Champagne. Oh, and for the record, Scotland haven't qualified for a major tournament since 1998.

With my dad being Scottish and a lot of my family being from Scotland, it was always awkward for me when it came to international football. I was born in Birmingham but when it came to tournaments, I sided with Scotland rather than England due to my family. I suppose you could say Scotland's most famous fan, Rod Stewart, isn't from Scotland either.

I went to my first Scotland game against Norway in 1989 and have been to Wembley twice in recent years to watch them play England. This was purely to take my dad down there. International football has lost its appeal for me over the years. With the Champions League taking priority these days, it's nowhere near as good. I still watch all the tournaments as a football fan, but it's nothing like club football for me. I actually dread it now when international weekend arrives, with teams like San Marino and Andorra on the TV when you're used to having a full programme on a normal weekend. I've got a lot of friends who feel exactly the same way.

I think the supporters of both the England and Scotland national teams have changed. When you see flags at away games, it's mostly small clubs who take big numbers away these days. I saw the England supporters at the World Cup in Russia and it now looks like a different breed.

Wembley is now a great stadium, as it should be with all the money that's been spent on it. Hampden was done on the cheap and is in need of a major facelift. I still want Hampden to stay, but they do do need to change the stands behind the goals and bring them closer to the pitch.

This fixture is still a big game, though. When you look back and think of all the quality players that have played through the years, it's worth saving. It will always have a place in people's hearts.

Belfast

Glentoran v Linfield
(April 23rd 2005)
'Big Two'

Top tips for Belfast
Going straight from a nightclub to an airport is never a good idea.
Be ready to witness violence on the pitch.
Be prepared to walk back to the city centre.
Never say you have come over to watch football when introduced to people on a night out.
If you have a Del Boy moment, play it cool.

This may not be the world's most glamorous derby, but for supporters of these clubs it means the world. Of the rivalries I've seen across the world, this was the game that had the most violence in the ground.

Most people hear the word Belfast and instantly have an image in their head of bombs, riots and violence. It is a city that is still on edge, but it's a different world to what it was during the Troubles. You find lots of tourists there now, doing tours up the Shankill and Falls Roads. It's also a popular place for stag and hen parties. I first went there in 1995 and the city has changed a lot. A lot of murals are becoming more sports influenced and people's attitudes have also changed.

When I was planning my travel arrangements for this particular weekend, I decided to really go for it. I was still living in Birmingham in 2005 and thought I'd have a nice quiet weekend – I say that with sarcasm. My itinerary was flying from Birmingham to Belfast Saturday morning, Belfast to Glasgow Sunday morning, and then a train from Glasgow to Birmingham Monday afternoon. The reason for the Glasgow part of the journey was to go to the Old Firm game on the Sunday lunchtime.

Linfield and Glentoran are big rivals and are Northern Ireland's two biggest teams historically and supporters' wise. A lot of people may think religion is a big reason for their rivalry but it isn't. Both clubs are predominantly Protestant and play in Protestant areas. Glentoran play at the Oval in East Belfast and most of their support comes from there. Linfield play at Windsor Park in South Belfast and draw most of their support from there and the Shankill area.

All derbies are big games but this one was bigger than normal. It was the penultimate game of the season and Linfield were one point ahead of Glentoran. They both had an easy fixture in their last match of the season the following weekend. So, in theory, if Linfield could win or draw, the title was theirs. It was a 12,000 sell out, which is a very big crowd for an Irish Premier League match.

A football team I was playing for in Birmingham had decided to have an end-of-season trip away to Belfast on the same weekend. My cousin Mathew and I met up with them once we had dropped our bags off at our hotel in the Sandy Row area. We headed for a few beers at the Raven Social Club in East Belfast, which has supporters from both teams that drink in there. There was some good banter flying about between them. A few of the older Linfield lads seemed really nervous, but it wasn't stopping them necking pints of Harp.

We made our way to the Welders Club, just off the Newtownards Road. It was really busy with Linfield fans. Mathew had got a few souvenirs from a nearby shop and he left them behind the bar to collect after the game. The Oval was only a short walk away in an area surrounded by loyalist murals. There was quite a long queue to get in and the kick-off was delayed by twenty minutes. With the sunny warm weather, it had a cup final day feel to it.

The Oval is an old-school football ground; it's got an open terrace at each end and two stands along the touchlines. It's also right next to Belfast City Airport. The planes are so low when coming in to land, it feels like a decent kick from the keeper could hit one of them.

With everybody packed in for this game, it had a good atmosphere. It was quite colourful, too, and the red, green and black of the Glens were easy to spot. The Linfield section was a sea of blue and white, with lots of snazzy headgear on show. We got a good spot on the corner of the open terrace and were up towards the back.

Before mentioning this game, I have to tell you that these teams are part-time footballers. They hold down normal jobs and train maybe two or three times a week. Obviously the standard isn't that high but the players give their all.

Glentoran were first out the traps and opened the scoring through Parkhouse. It was quite nervy but the Blues equalised through McAreavy. While the game was being played at a fast pace, I noticed a few missiles being thrown from both sides in the far corner. Linfield fans were throwing them from the Old Shed, while the Glens were throwing them at the corner of the Sydenham End.

I was bursting for a piss at this stage, and me and Mathew headed for the toilet just before half-time. I say toilet – everybody was just standing on the grass verge having a piss. The facilities were very basic, to put it mildly. After relieving myself, I started to lose my footing and rolled down the verge towards the fence. Mathew turned round in mid-sentence and wondered where I'd gone. Think of Del Boy and Trigger in *Only Fools and Horses*. I tried to act all cool but the grass stain on my jeans gave the game away.

Linfield started the second half well but the Glens scored against the run of play through Nixon. The longer the game went on, I was sure Linfield weren't going to score. With four minutes remaining, the Blues equalised from a long punt up the park that substitute Larmour scored from. Cue lots of jubilation, Linfield had effectively won the league.

The missiles were now raining down from disgruntled Glens fans at the Sydenham End. The police moved in to try and force a no-man's land and keep a distance between the two sets of fans. With all this happening in the background, the match was still being played and the Glens somehow scored the winning goal out of nothing through Morgan. The ball slowly trickled over the line, to the agony of the Blues players. As football games go, that was a fucking mental few minutes.

The final whistle blew to scenes of pandemonium. With players still on the park and some totally gutted, the Blues fans ran through a gate and onto the pitch. I didn't think this would last for long, but I was totally wrong. More Blues fans came on to the pitch and started challenging the Glens to come and join them – and it wasn't for a cup of tea and biscuits. Bottles were thrown down from the main stand at the Blues fans. As soon as one would come down, then another one would head in the opposite direction.

This went on for a few minutes until the Glens eventually forced a gate open and charged on to the pitch. After this there were battles galore: fists were flying and a few heads were getting whacked like a football. While this was happening, bottles were still being thrown down. It felt like an age before the police finally restored some order and the fans slowly went back to terraces. What was all the more remarkable was that it was being filmed live on the BBC.

We were slowly making our way to the exit when a fan hit a police officer over the head with a big stick. Nobody batted an eyelid; it felt like the world had gone mad for twenty minutes.

We'd intended to head back to the Welders Club and collect Mathew's souvenir bag but it wasn't possible. The Glens had blocked off the road and the police were insisting we went the other way. So after the madness, we walked in to the city centre alongside the motorway. A few of my pals started phoning me, saying there had been news about the trouble on Sky Sports, which was unusual for an Irish Premier game.

We had a function to attend at the start of the evening back over in the east of the city. It was like being at a funeral for some of the Linfield fans there. They knew Glentoran would be champions. I felt gutted for the lads who go and support them every week. We didn't stay for too long.

We got taxis to Benedict's bar in the city centre. If I was being sensible, I would have had a few more beers and then got a decent sleep before my early-morning flight to Glasgow. Not one for being sensible, I headed to a nightclub near the famous City Hall called Thompson's. It's a late club, where people who are there are bang on it. When a guy asked me, 'Why are you in Belfast?', I told him, 'To watch Linfield,' which he wasn't too happy about. There were a few of us there and he went away talking to himself. At half four, with the tunes blasting, I realised I'd soon need to get my bag from my hotel and head to the International Airport with Mathew.

We made our flight to Glasgow and watched Celtic win the Old Firm derby with Craig Bellamy scoring the winning goal. With no sleep, my batteries finally ran out and my weekend was over.

Glentoran fans still call this game 'Morgan Day', and they won the league the following Saturday. The IFA had an inquest into the scenes after the final whistle. It just goes to show what can happen at a derby no matter what the level of football. Whether it's 12,000 or 80,000 in attendance, your derby is your derby.

Hamburg

Would I ever get to this fixture? Ever since I went there in 2011 for the called-off game, I've kept my eye on this game entering the fixture list. For this to happen, St Pauli would need to get promoted again or Hamburg get relegated. I hadn't been back to Hamburg since, but had seen them play at Hertha Berlin in 2014. Considering they used to be one of the giants of the Bundesliga, it was sad to see their demise into a very average team, but still backed by full houses every home game and with a big away following.

Everybody knows about the clock at the Volksparkstadion ticking away for the time Hamburg have been in the Bundesliga, but it was getting more precarious with every passing year. They survived play off scares in 2014 and again in 2015. They also had a last day escape at home in 2017. The club was in a mess on and off the park.

On the 12th May 2018, Hamburg finally got relegated. It felt like putting an old dog to sleep. Despite winning their game at home against Monchengladbach, other results went against them and for the first time in almost fifty-five years, Hamburg would not be playing in the Bundesliga. I had been keeping an eye on their results and at one stage it looked like St Pauli would get relegated as well. It felt like this game would never happen. They eventually stayed up and would be renewing hostilities at the start of 2018/19 season.

I turned forty in 2018 and had a planned a few weekends away. My fortieth was in Belfast at the start of September with my mates so, to be honest, when the fixture list came out I was hoping this would be later in the year. My girlfriend had asked me where I fancied going for a weekend. I told her the story about how long I'd been waiting to go to this game and, after a quick roll of her eyes, she agreed to a weekend in Hamburg.

The logistics of this trip were pretty straightforward. We booked from Edinburgh to Hamburg on Saturday morning and were returning Sunday evening. The game was being played Sunday afternoon. It was an early morning flight, so we stayed at an hotel at

Edinburgh Park on Friday evening. I'd arranged match tickets from 'H' back in Scotland, but we had to pick them up on the match day. Surely this game wouldn't get called off or abandoned, or the flights cancelled?

I was actually looking forward to seeing a bit of Hamburg this time. We hadn't left the Reeperbahn district last time and my diet had consisted of Burger King meals. I was planning on having at least one nice meal this time. There were a few familiar faces on the flight over. By the sounds of things, the Reeperbahn was going to be wild again.

In the build-up to this match there were a few incidents involving both Ultras groups. HSV Ultras disrupted a concert involving bands linked to St Pauli. St Pauli Ultras then returned the favour by disrupting their rivals' choreography preparations, injuring two HSV Ultras in the process.

After this happened, there were a few hanging effigies from bridges across the city with bags of straw and St Pauli's colours of red, white and brown painted on them. The pot was bubbling nicely.

To simplify this derby, I would say that Hamburg is the big, powerful, established club. Some St Pauli fans would say that HSV is a right-wing club, which is nonsense. Most clubs in Germany have an element of right-wing supporters. St Pauli is a left-wing club and has became trendy with some folk for its anti-racist and anti-fascist principles. A lot of fans say they are against commercialism but they open up club shops with their skull and crossbone logo. Personally, I think they don't know what direction they want their club to go in. It's a lot clearer with Hamburg; they must get back in the Bundesliga asap and sort all their shit out off the park.

We went down to the port area and had a decent meal. There were lots of families enjoying their day out, but I couldn't help wondering what the Reeperbahn would be like later on.

After a few beers, my girlfriend wanted to see this famous area as it was her first time in Hamburg. After a slow walk up there, I noticed the area had improved since the last time I'd been there. There were more bars and restaurants up at the top end. The bars were lively, as you'd expect, and it wasn't just groups of lads either.

As it was starting to get dark, police were deployed on every corner linking the red-light district to the Reeperbahn. On Hans-

Albers-Platz, just by the London pub, it seemed they were expecting confrontation. We carried on drinking in a few other bars. At that stage I was pissed and needing my bed. We were staying just by the Central Station, so it was only a short taxi ride. It seemed like the police learnt their lessons from 2011 and there weren't any major disturbances on the eve of the game.

After a quick breakfast, we got the train for Stellingen, which is the nearest stop to the Volksparkstadion. The guy with our tickets was meeting us there; there were also various bars set up. The Tankstelle sports bar had a stool there, and we met up with the rest of the lads. There are courtesy buses that take you to the ground, but we walked the fifteen-minute journey. I'd heard that St Pauli were having a fan march to the stadium. They had 6,000 tickets and marched together, all wearing white T-shirts.

The ground is at the end of a forest but there are fan parks set up with barbecues and bars. We were in Block 28, and would be on the corner of the Nordtribune where the HSV Ultras were.

The pre-match atmosphere was really good and with the tannoy system being played at full blast, it felt like a rock concert. The St Pauli fans were diagonally across from us and let off a constant stream of flares to start with. This was my first time in this stadium and I was well impressed. There was plenty of legroom and not a bad view to be had anywhere inside. The HSV Ultras have a standing section and that was rocking. Both teams came out to great tifo displays from both supports, and the ground was buzzing.

I was looking forward to seeing this game at last. It was a 57,000 sell out for a second-tier game, which was incredible. I was also looking forward to seeing the Ginger Ramos aka David Bates, and hopefully a few goals.

The game was probably the flattest I've been at. The quality of the football was very poor. I admired the Ultras who sang all through it, but this was a major anti-climax. We were all expecting fireworks but at times it felt like a pre-season friendly.

Some of the lads left at half-time and went back to the Reeperbahn. We stayed till around five minutes from the end. When we were walking back to the station, we heard a big roar. It turned out that a St Pauli player had tried to chip the HSV goalkeeper from inside his own half but it was just about turned over the bar. That one thing was the highlight of the whole game.

We jumped on the train and within thirty minutes we were sitting having a drink overlooking the canal. People around us were completely unaware of the football game that had divided the city's football fans. I started seeing a few things on my phone regarding the game. HSV had left stink bombs on the train platform for when the St Pauli fans were disembarking before their fan march. If that wasn't bad enough, piles of human excrement were left for them outside the away entrance. Some fans were actually physically sick at the smell. Not your average Sunday.

After a few more drinks in the centre, we made our way to the airport. A few of the lads were telling me that water cannons were being deployed around the Reeperbahn in case of any trouble later. If I'm being totally honest, I was expecting much more from this game. Everything was set up for a great game but it fell flat. At least I finally made it but hopefully Hamburg will only last one season in this league.

Birmingham

Birmingham City v Aston Villa
(December 12th 1987)
'Second city derby'

It's a typical Saturday in December. People are heading out shopping for presents and putting decorations up. I'm nine years of age and heading to my first-ever football derby – and it's a big one.

As you probably know by now, I'm a Rangers' fan although born and bred in Birmingham. When I was younger I would also go and watch Aston Villa with friends and family. I wasn't sure whether my dad would take me to this game, due to the potential for violence.

In 1987 there weren't shiny, all-seating arenas and the Premier League was a pipe-dream. Most grounds were shitholes and were falling apart, but they did have character. You were lucky if somebody came round selling cartons of juice or packets of crisps. A lot of people never bothered fighting their way to the back of the terrace to the toilet either. Some would simply piss right next to where they were standing, or head to the front and piss up against the fence. The fences were quite high and designed to keep you penned in and not on the pitch; welcome to the eighties. To think people going to games nowadays moan about the wi-fi reception.

This game was in the old second division, Villa had been relegated the previous season from the first division. The two teams had met in August and Birmingham had won the game 2–0. Tickets were no issue for this game as it was pay at the gate. The only problem with paying at the gate was that you had to be there early to guarantee entry. Once the away section was full, the gates would then be closed. It was a 3pm kick-off on a Saturday afternoon.

This derby may not be as glamorous as a North London, Manchester or a Merseyside derby, but it's still a big game in the second city. West Bromwich Albion, Wolves and Coventry make the Midlands a decent area for football rivalry, but this is the main game for both sets of fans.

The city centre could be a lively spot after these games. Birmingham's Zulus' firm were always out in numbers and had a reputation, especially in the eighties. Villa's firm were the C Crew and always turned out in numbers for this fixture. And Villa Park and St Andrews are only two miles apart.

A lot of Villa fans were drinking in their normal match-day boozers, due to the close proximity of the two grounds. We were in the Manor Tavern in Aston; this was a pub where I was allowed in. Standing outside for two hours in December wouldn't have been great.

The game got mentioned on the TV programme *Saint and Greavsie*, while in this pub there were rumours going around about the C Crew and Zulus having it off by the big fire station in town. It's mad how I can remember little things like that from more than thirty years ago, but I couldn't tell you what I was doing yesterday morning.

We eventually made our way to St Andrews by taxi and were greeted with a queue that was snaking down the street. We got to the turnstiles and I was squeezed in free of charge. I'm sure most young lads back in the day experienced this.

Five years before this game in the old division two, Aston Villa had won the European Cup. It's crazy now when you look back at that statistic. There were actually two players in this game who'd played in that final against Bayern Munich: Nigel Spink was playing in goal for Villa, and Des Bremner was now playing for the Blues and coming to the end of his career. Two young defenders by the names of Julian Dicks and Martin Keown were also playing, and the talented Mark Walters was there in one of his last games, with his famous double shuffle. Villa were managed by Graham Taylor and the Blues by Garry Pendrey.

There were a few incidents before kick-off at the corner flag, despite there being a segregation fence. It was weird seeing people getting arrested before the game and being marched past us to the main stand. We were in the Tilton Road end, with the bulk of the Blues support in the Spion Kop. Both of these were terraced sections. The main stand and the railway end were both seated. There were 28,000 at this game, which wasn't a bad crowd for that era.

I'd love to tell you that this was a lovely end-to-end football match but from my memory it was a battle. You could get away with a lot more tackling-wise in those days. Villa took the lead when

Garry Thompson scored a header from a Kevin Gage cross up at the railway end. Birmingham equalised with a bizarre goal through Andy Kennedy. He struck a great shot low into the corner of Nigel Spinks' goal, but there was a hole in the net and the ball was heading in our direction as he was running towards the Kop with his hand in the air. So you had three sides of the ground celebrating and a match ball ending up at the corner flag. It was a perfectly good goal and the atmosphere went up a few notches.

Villa scored the winning goal late on in the second half through another Garry Thompson header. He beat Vince Overson in the air to bullet home a header from another Kevin Gage cross. That was great if you were a Villa fan, but not so good for my brand-new blue Reebok Classics, which were now black and wet. There were more skirmishes over at the corner at the Spion Kop before the referee blew the full-time whistle.

I do remember my dad taking me in to a nearby bookmakers straight from the game and it was probably a wise decision. I would like to think we we went there and waited till things calmed down outside but, knowing my dad, it might have been to see how his football coupon had got on and how many losing horses he'd backed during the day on his place spot.

While in this bookies, the constant sound of police sirens nearby was worrying for a nine year old. When we eventually came out the area was deserted. We headed to get a bus home and away from the city centre to get the *Sports Argos*. This was a pink sports paper and was like a bible for football fans on a Saturday evening. There were various different types of Saturday sports paper all over Britain at that time.

Although we never witnessed any major violence at the game, the *Sunday Mercury* was full of reports of violence from the previous day. A pub near the away section had seen all its windows smashed. There had also been trouble in the city centre.

Villa would get promoted to the first division at the end of this season. Birmingham would endure years of turmoil with the Kumar brothers taking over; the less said about them the better. The two teams would not play each other in a league game again until September 2002. That's a very long time to wait for a derby. There were cup clashes in between. In fact, a good pal of mine called Paul

Tait got sent off at Villa Park in 1994 for throwing the then Villa captain, Kevin Richardson, into the Trinity Road Stand.

I have friends and family on both sides of this rivalry. When they play there's always potential for trouble. I grew up in the Kingshurst area and there were always incidents when these two teams played. I would call it a ninety-minute hatred for your average fan; most people get on with each other a few hours after the game, and work alongside each other.

Sutton Coldfield is a big Villa area and Chelmsley Wood is still a big Blues area. There is a lot of banter that flies about, which can turn nasty every now and again. Their two firms share a hatred of each other and that will never go away. I know lads from both firms and they are good decent lads.

At the time of writing this book, both clubs are in the championship, which is sad to see. The second city should always be represented in the Premier League. Hopefully both teams will go up soon. They both have good supports, but won't get promoted on history alone.

Football now seems completely different to what it was back in 1987. Players were not on megabucks back then, and seemed a lot closer with the fans. Hopefully football doesn't sell its soul too much in this new era. The games always have an early kick-off now, and are almost always played on a Sunday. This is on police advice, as the games are sometimes not televised. Fans getting locked in after the game is now accepted as normal.

Not a bad game for your first derby. Yes, there are much bigger derbies, but for both sets of supporters on that day, their derby was all that mattered to them.

Afterword

Writing this book has felt like being in therapy at times when looking back at some of these games. From going to games as a young boy to going with different partners on some of these trips, it's been a journey through my life.

Players for these clubs will always come and go, but the fans are still there and the colours of their shirts remain the same. These games still generate the same passion and loud voices from the stands. Teams will have their ups and downs, but a victory over your biggest rivals is always one of the sweetest and best feelings in football.

Boca v River made headlines in the Copa Libertadores Final in 2018, with the game eventually getting played in Madrid. Away fans arc still banned in Argentina. Red Star made the group stages of the Champions League for the first time, and did well considering the standard of opposition. Genoa and Sampdoria fans had to deal with a major bridge collapsing in their city, which was tragic. Rangers and Celtic are still battling away in the madness of Scottish football. The big two in Belfast now have competition from other teams. Barca v Real Madrid is still one of the most watched matches in the world. Sporting Lisbon had a crazy few months after my visit, but things seem back to normal now. Curva Nord and Curva Sud still hold a lot of power in Rome. Milan and Inter are slowly coming back to strength, after a few years in the doldrums, but currently remain in Juventus's shadow.

I've made some good friends whilst going to some of these games. The people who have helped with tickets, I can't thank you enough. It always makes life so much easier if you aren't chasing about for tickets. There are some games that I've looked forward to, more so than others but they've all been good in their own way. The crowd has been more interesting than the actual football at most of these games. Pyro, tifo and good old-fashioned singing make these occasions all the better.

I still plan to go to more derbies in the future and have a list of potential ones in my head. I hope this book was a decent read for you – and thanks for buying it.

Games Featured

Boca Juniors v River Plate (1–1)

Racing Club v Velez Sarsfield (0–0)

Real Madrid v Barcelona (0–4)

Red Star v Partizan (0–2)

Lazio v Roma (0–1)

Genoa v Sampdoria (0–1)

Celtic v Rangers (3–1)

Inter v Milan (0–1)

Glentoran v Linfield (3–2)

England v Scotland (0–1)

Hamburg v St Pauli (0–0)

Republic of Ireland v Northern Ireland (0–0)

Birmingham City v Aston Villa (1–2)

Sporting Lisbon v Benfica (0–0)

Feyenoord v Ajax (6–2)

Acknowledgements

These trips were done with the help of some great people. Some of the banter was top notch; if only all the stories were printable. Some of you had to endure my terrible gags as well.

A special thanks goes to Davie Blair from Bridgeton for producing the magic pieces of paper for me and my family for thirty years. I'm also grateful to: Big Longboy for finally recognising me in the Tankstelle; Hunter for sorting Hamburg twice; Marco from Rotterdam; Mikey from the Shankill; Mike for his hospitality in Hamburg; Stuart in BA; Digger for the advice and help, and Blucky for Wembley 1999. Also my dad, for brainwashing me and taking me to my first games. It's been emotional...

Printed in Great Britain
by Amazon

36104059R00056